Holding On by a Thread

Thread

A Trans Memoir

Stefonknee (Paul) Wolscht

Dedication

I'd like to dedicate Holding On by a Thread to my children and my grandchildren, who through their love and acceptance have given me new purpose in life. Chavonne, Amanda, Christopher, Michael, Nicole, Peter and Robert, you are the meaning of life to me, and I cannot express in words how much I love you and appreciate you being the amazing people that you are. I'm extremely proud of you and everything that you've accomplished with your lives. You make this world a better place.

I would also like to dedicate this book to my mother and father, Mary Lou and Paul as well as my siblings Monica, Michael, Eric, and Robert and their wonderful families.

Being the transgender child in the family has presented many challenges for each of us, I pray that we have all grown and learned from the experience and are now able to share our love as a family for the rest of the days that we get to spend on this planet.

(((((((Hugs))))))) Stefonknee

Acknowledgement

I would like to first acknowledge the support and protection that I received through The Gerstein Crisis Centre, Street Haven at the Crossroads women's shelter, St. Michael's Hospital, Mount Sinai Hospital, CAMH, St. Joseph's Hospital, Peterborough Regional Health Centre, Toronto Western Hospital, and MCC Toronto Church while I struggled with depression and homelessness. You were there to help me and protect me when all I could feel was extreme sadness.

I would also like to acknowledge that the hope that I found in life has come to realization because of the words of my granddaughter. She changed my world forever and I love you to infinity and beyond plus one. ((((Hugs)))) Opa

Contents

Chapter 1

St. Mike's Hospital

Who decided that a canary should be a canary?

July 23, 2009

I'm sitting on a small bed in the emergency department at St. Michael's Hospital, panicking. The steel door to my room is open. A security guard is seated directly opposite, on suicide watch.

I'm crying and shaking uncontrollably. My mind keeps replaying the previous forty-eight hours over and over again, desperate to see what I could have done differently.

I was losing everything that had ever given me security, everything and everyone that made me happy. I had chosen to risk it all and there was no safety net to protect me. I was scared, more scared than I had ever been. My situation felt hopeless.

How could I get out of the mess I'd gotten myself into? I wished I could just disappear and die. I desperately needed the doctors to help me stop hating myself. I had to find something, anything, to give me some hope.

I had had hope all my adult life. I had been happily married for Twenty-Three-years and we'd been loving and raising seven wonderful children together. I had worked hard to become a respected businessman in my community, a pillar in my church and a valued, contributing member of society on many levels. I had

1

finished my schooling, worked hard, and earned everything that gave me a secure, happy middle-class lifestyle, or so I thought.

Paul Wolscht working from home at PAW Service

All along the way, those seven children had been my main reason for existing, the prime source of my joy. With the help of relatives, I had built a beautiful home on the sandy banks of the Black River in the quiet hamlet of Elm Grove. I had moved my mechanic shop into the huge, attached garage I had purposely built so I could be there with my kids, morning, noon, and night.

I was increasingly a part of the community through my children's sports and recreation, sitting on various boards and committees, and being active in local politics. Our family was constantly involved in volunteering, fundraising, and helping to organize events everywhere we went. Always our beautiful children filled our home with love. Those were the best years of my life.

Back Row: Christopher, Maria, Amanda, Michael. Middle Row: Robert, Chavonne, Rebecca, Peter. Front Row: Jacob and Nicole. The Wolscht Family

How did I lose that beautiful life?

I had one big, underlying problem. From early childhood I had wanted to be a girl. With the support of my mother and later my wife, Maria, I'd managed to keep my secret for over forty years. My need to stop hiding my identity as a woman kept escalating to the point where I had to come out of the closet and be true to myself. Maria gave me an ultimatum, "Stop being transgender or leave." Brashly, I packed a bag and left for Toronto.

I just never realized how devastating my actions would be.

My actions impacted everyone I knew with a domino effect that made them feel personally violated by my having revealed my secret. Life at home in Elm Grove would never be the same again for my wife or my children. And I found myself in downtown Toronto, feeling rejected and heartbroken, under suicide watch.

Little did I know then that things would get so much worse. I'd not only lose my house but also my shop and business. That I'd find myself homeless and penniless, cut off from all funds and assets. And, worst of all, I wouldn't see my children for the next decade. What I had heard was happening to other trans people was now happening to me.

Earlier that day I had bought three bottles of Tylenol and left my room in a friend's apartment. I prepared to go to a park somewhere and, take the pills and slowly fall asleep, to never have to wake up again. My only thought was to stop the pain and move on to whatever awaits us in the afterlife. The last thing to do was to meet my dear friend, Eve, who was expecting me to join her for dinner in Kensington Market at a quiet Chinese restaurant.

Despite my attempt to act normal, Eve asked me, "What's wrong?"

That's when I broke down and started crying. I told her my secret that I'd lost my children and my home, and I wanted to die. She refused to let me go home alone without first getting an assessment by a doctor. St. Michael's Hospital turned out to be where I ended up. How? I don't know. I can't remember anything about the ride over except that I was crying.

I'm not sure how long I remained in Emerg, but eventually, I woke up in a warm bed. The room was dark, and I was cotton-mouthed and confused. I made my way out to the nurses' station to get something to drink. Alone in the dark corridor, cold and embarrassed, I leaned against the wall, waiting for the charge nurse to take notice of me. The sign on the window to the nursing station read "Knocking on the glass will NOT help us serve you faster." I waited for what felt like an hour. I saw the reflection of her computer screen on the darkened window behind her. She was busy posting pictures to a Facebook account.

I remember whimpering in the dark. I don't know for how long. I was heartbroken and depressed, and I felt helpless. She finally slid the glass open and I asked her for some water. There I was, standing in a dark corridor, completely helpless, asking someone with "power" for something as simple as a glass of water. She left into the dark room behind her, emerging a few moments later with a paper cup full of ice water. I thanked her, emptied the cup into my dry mouth and left the nurses' station. Back in my bed, unable to sleep, I wrestled with my thoughts for the rest of the night. I stared at the ceiling, and I kept wondering, How did I get myself into this mess?! Exhausted and tired, I drifted off to sleep again.

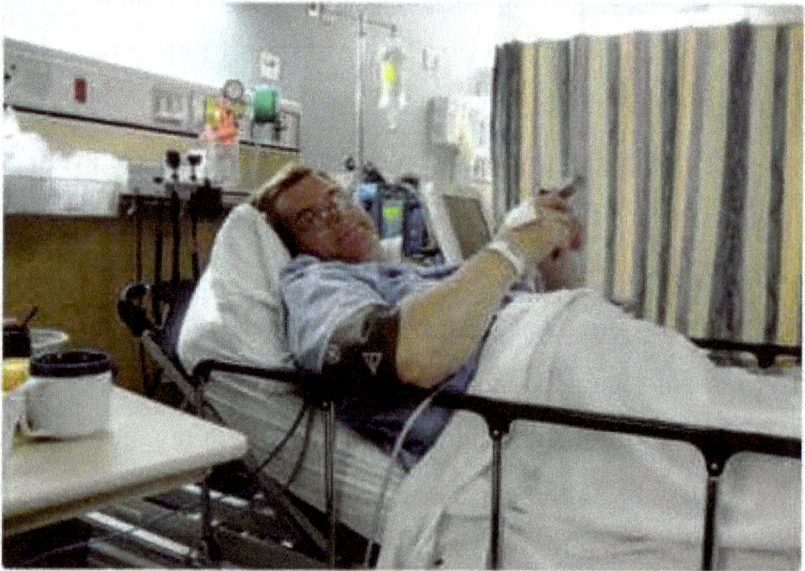

In my room at St. Michael's Hospital, Toronto. (July 24/09)

Four hospital staff entered my room soon after, and I was introduced to Dr. Robinson, Dr. Ooi and two nurses, Sonya and

Heather. They understood that I had come to the hospital voluntarily the day before. They wanted to schedule a time to hear my story, in my own words, of what brought me to the hospital and what I hoped to achieve during my stay at St. Mike's. How could I know what I was hoping to achieve when I had thoughts of hopelessness and suicide? I came here to be cured, and if they could just give me some medication to fix my depression, I'd be on my way back into the city to figure things out.

Later that afternoon, I met with Dr. Ooi and Dr. Robinson, and they asked me exactly what had happened to make me want to take my life. I told them that my wife, Maria, no longer accepted my transgender identity and had given me a choice: "Either stop being transgender or leave."

I didn't know what to do: if I stayed with her, I would have to throw away my clothes and stop expressing my feminine side, but if I left, I would lose my children, my house, my job, everything and everyone that I loved. It seemed like an impossible choice: stay and be trapped for the rest of my life, or leave and lose everything. I knew I was transgender and that would never change, but I needed to know that I could live my authentic truth and be free to express myself without the threat of being punished for being me. Hoping to keep the peace, I packed a couple of bags of clothes and left my home, figuring I could come back after a few days.

I opened up to Dr. Robertson and Dr. Ooi and began telling

them about my past. I went all the way back to when I had first met Maria DiMambro. I was friends with her older brother, Carlo, and she would sometimes come to watch our pickup ball hockey games on the blacktop behind Mount Albert Public School in a small town north of Toronto. I didn't realize that she had a crush on me. I was totally oblivious to girls' feelings. My sexuality and gender identity left me wondering if I were gay or straight. I was very insecure about my sexuality and whatever it was that caused me to be attracted to wearing feminine clothes. At that time, I had never heard the term transgender or gender expression. Having a girlfriend would somehow make things easier by hiding the fact that I was sexually insecure, and it allowed me to explore those feelings. Looking back, I think being in a heterosexual relationship helped calm my fear of being exposed and helped me keep my secret hidden.

Maria and I kept dating throughout her high school years and the years of my auto mechanic apprenticeship. Three years later, we became sexually active for the first time. She was my first sexual partner, and I wasn't sure if having sex with her would make me "normal." I knew it felt good to have a girlfriend, someone I could confide in—it made me feel mature and in control of the confusion in my mind. One evening late that summer, Maria saw me browsing through a Sears catalogue while sitting on her bed. I was looking in the women's section, specifically looking at lingerie. She became very angry and considered my looking at half-dressed women as a form of pornography. I explained to her that I wasn't looking at the women. Rather, I felt like a woman and was looking at the clothes they were wearing. My mind raced as I said it out loud; she was the only person in the world, other than my mom, who knew that I had an attraction to all things feminine.

I then waited to see if she would accept me or be upset and reveal my secret to her friends and family. Maria came home the next day with a gift for me: a grey panty and camisole set, a white blouse and a black pleated skirt, and said she would help me with my cross-dressing. It could not have gone any better.

At that point, my heart melted. It felt amazing to realize and know that she could love me and accept me for who I was, completely and unconditionally. I'm not sure if what I was feeling was love or just unconditional acceptance, but what I do know is my life changed that day, and with Maria, I had a chance to start letting my little girl inside my head come out and express herself.

Our shopping trips to buy women's clothes would continue for the next couple of years as we dated. We also started going on dates to Toronto, to a club called Take a Walk on the Wildside, a cross-dressers' store in the heart of the city where I could dress as a girl. It was at that time that we decided that my fem name should be Stephanie. Stephanie was free at last, and that made Maria and me happy. Stephanie had lived too long in my head and away from the light of day. I started to take chances and reveal more and more of my inner girl.

We continued dating for the next year and a half until the summer of 1986. On the May 24 weekend, Maria and I were in the park in Mount Albert with a group of friends, waiting for the Victoria Day fireworks to begin. It was hot and very muggy, and Maria seemed a bit distracted. What happened next took me totally by surprise. She introduced me to her "other boyfriend," John Doucette. She had decided to play "eenie, meanie, mynie, moe" with her two boyfriends in order to choose who she would keep dating. We both stood there like fools, letting her treat us like inanimate objects. Maria chose John. I was heartbroken and scared again that what secrets we had would be made public. I left the park immediately, shedding crocodile tears, not out of grief but more of feeling that I was now free to live my life as Stephanie full time and inquire about having a sex change. Actually, what did I have to lose if I changed and became Stephanie? I would be revealing my secret not Maria, and I would be in control of my life again.

These thoughts did not last very long because, by the following Saturday, I was told that Maria was in the hospital; she had attempted to end her life. I visited her in the hospital in Newmarket, only to find out that she had been testing me. When she chose John, she expected me to get jealous and fight for her love. When I didn't and just moved on with my life, she felt that she had gambled too much and had lost everything. Little did I know that this is part of her personality; she manipulates others into feeling guilty for not letting her have her own way. I'm not sure what happened to John or what she had told him; all I knew was he was now out of the picture, and I was standing there responsible for her suicide attempt.

Knowing she had attempted suicide, I felt guilty and decided that I would start dating her again to keep her safe. We were sexually active again and began talking about settling down together and getting married in the summer of 1987. This flew in the face of my plans to set Stephanie free and become a girl, and it put me back into the world of pretending that I was happy as a man. It didn't take very long before Maria told me that she was pregnant and thought we should get married that December before she started showing. I felt trapped, but I felt responsible for getting us pregnant and bringing this life into the world. I was backed into a corner and feared Stephanie would forever remain deep inside of me.

Paul and Maria Wolscht (December 27, 1986)

I felt frustrated and angry at myself because I had caused this by starting to date her again and by having unprotected sex. How could I have been so stupid? In the end, we got married on December

27, 1986, and the following June, we welcomed our first child, Chavonne, into the world.

Back in my room, I met my social worker and, thank God, we talked about some of my unresolved issues. The social worker on my team took on the task of looking into another issue that had brought me to the hospital. I was still on the hook for a real estate deal, a property that I had been hoping to buy before everything went south. It was meant to be a home for me as well as my new business, a transgender/lesbian bar called "StefZ Twisted Candy Factory" in a building at 781 Queen St. East, just past Broadview Avenue, in Toronto. This real estate deal that was supposed to close in a week was now in shambles. Maria would only release the $51,000 deposit if I signed a separation agreement that stated I would not present as female or wear women's clothes in public. I was given legal advice not to sign it as I would be signing away my human rights. I had already put down a $40,000 deposit that emptied my bank account. I only had $700 to my name and no job to go to for work. That is what led me to consider suicide: I was desperate, and I had enough life insurance that I could close the deal after I died. I know what you're thinking and you're right: I would be dead, and it wouldn't work, but at that time, it made sense to me.

In my next session with Dr. Ooi and Dr. Robertson, we discussed my life as a cross-dresser and father, married to Maria, and that we had our second baby, Amanda, in July 1988. The year after that, we had a miscarriage. That scared us because we thought that we were going too fast, and Maria's body needed a break. Two years later, we welcomed our son Christopher into the world. I felt so alive as we raised our children; it felt like I was a good mom as well as a dad. During this time, I was working as a mechanic during the day and delivering newspapers at night to rural Georgina and East Gwillimbury in York Region for extra income to put Maria through school. Maria was still a student at York University when she had our fourth child, Michael. After that, she began teaching, and we ended up having three more babies—Nicole, Peter, and finally, Robert in December 1998. Seven kids in eleven years. For the next fifteen years, I got to be a mom to these amazing little kids while working from home as a mechanic. I cannot describe the joy that I felt when these gifts from God looked lovingly into my eyes. I couldn't have been happier and life felt perfect. Perfect, except that I was hiding the girl inside of me and only bringing her out in the bedroom or at night in Toronto. Life seemed perfect, but I was scared and living a lie.

Weekly Sunday Brunch at the Wolscht House

A few days later, while I was in group therapy, my father and Maria came to talk to my doctors. Although I didn't know it at the time, they convinced them that I was not only depressed but had episodes of mania as well. I was put on a high dose of Seroquel, so high that my tongue felt numb, and I sometimes had trouble talking. I found myself disassociating more, and many times, I couldn't remember what had happened moments earlier. I hated being on Seroquel– I felt it was utterly impossible to function as a human being, and I could in no way start my life over if I was on this medication.

The next day, Rick Tracey, a retired police officer from our church, brought Amanda, Chris, Nicole, Peter and Robert to Toronto to visit me. My kids met me in the TV room and we chatted for a bit. It was so embarrassing having them see me like this. Not only was I in the psych ward, but I couldn't form sentences or express how I was feeling. It was nice visiting with them, but I couldn't help thinking that they were afraid of me. I tried to remain focused and calm, but my mind drifted off and I can't remember what we talked about. The kids had to leave early to go and meet Rick to head back up to Sutton because he didn't want to get caught in traffic, and I was sent back to my room to rest, alone once again. It had been six weeks since I had officially moved out of the house. I was starting to piece together what was happening at home over the last two months and came to the realization that my marriage was over, that our family was going to split up and I was really on my own, displaced in a big cold city like Toronto.

Paul, Chris, Robert, Peter, Nicole, Michael and Amanda Wolscht

As I lay in my hospital bed, my mind swirling with the thoughts of my kids' visit, Dr. Robinson and Dr. Ooi entered my room to tell me some bad news, something about CAS (Children's Aid Society) and my having lost access to my children. I panicked and asked if I was free to leave the hospital. I found out that Dr. Robinson had called CAS. I was really angry and desperate to find a lawyer or go to the police. They told me that I was there of my own accord and that I was free to leave, so in a rush, I gathered up my stuff and decided to head to a police station to clarify why I was being separated from my children. What could I have done wrong to initiate this action? Everything was falling apart. I couldn't think straight, I couldn't speak properly, and I was trapped in Toronto, an hour's drive away from my kids.

I was heading out the front door of the hospital when three security guards approached me and asked me if my name was Stephanie Wolscht. They told me I had to go back up to the 17th floor with them. Shaking and in tears, I begged them to let me go to the police or call a lawyer to straighten out this mess. They basically told me that I could come voluntarily, or they would handcuff me and force me into the hospital. I broke down and reluctantly went back upstairs with them. It felt like I was a prisoner. I felt trapped and scared, and I didn't know what was happening. The doctors must have panicked and feared that I was acting irrationally.

Once I was back upstairs, I was taken into "The Dark Side" of the crisis unit, the half without doorknobs. I was really angry about this turn of events and began a hunger strike, not only to fight this injustice but also because I really wanted to die. Shortly afterwards, Dr. Ooi brought me a paper that said that they had placed me on Form 1 and that I was no longer a voluntary patient. I was locked in Room 106 of the crisis unit, stripped of all my clothes and kept there with nothing more than my underwear on. How could I have fallen so far? What happened to the person that I was only a few weeks ago? What was happening to me?

The reason that I panicked when Children's Aid got involved

is because back in 2003 while teaching grade nine Communication Technology at Our Lady of the Lake Catholic High School, there was an incident I could never forget. One of my rougher students, Jason, tried to pick a fight in the hall with a French teacher after school. I had heard the commotion and quickly moved to break up the attack when he threw a punch at my face. I caught his fist with my right hand and spun him around to walk him to the office. The principal let him leave while I filled out an incident report in the office with our vice-principal. Why was I in the office filling out this stupid paperwork and Jason was on his way home as if nothing had happened? The next day, the police were there when I finished work to tell me that I had injured Jason the previous day. I went to the police station to fill out a report with a CAS worker, Judy Edmonston. The police let me off, but the CAS worker got involved and started her own investigation. She made our life a living hell for the next few months. A few days after the incident, a police officer called me to come to the police station to read Judy's police file. Apparently, she had had many violent encounters with her own mother and her daughters that had warranted police interventions. Years later, she was investigated because of another incident like mine, where she blamed a supply teacher for something that was in her job description. It made the news and caused Judy to lose her job. My experience with her is what frightened me, triggering my fears that CAS could make my life worse than it already was. How was I going to regain control in all of this chaos?

I don't remember too much about my stay in the crisis unit. All I know is that eventually, I was moved back to the 17th-floor "regular inpatient" section and was introduced to some of the therapists who ran group therapy.

One of the women on our floor, Andrea, was not able to communicate with staff or other patients. I found out that she was getting shock therapy twice a day, which left her in a zombie state, sitting on the floor staring off into nothing.

That night, I woke up as usual, alone in my room after having a really weird dream. I dreamt that God told me to put my hand on the wall between Andrea's room and mine. When I touched the wall, my room got really cold, cold enough that I could see my breath. While touching the wall, I prayed for Andrea that I might somehow take the demons that were inside of her mind and free her from the hell she was in.

When I woke up the next morning, I told my nurse, Tatiana, what had happened, and she told me it wasn't a dream. She said that I had actually gone to the nursing station and reported that my room was really cold. They called maintenance once they entered my room and felt how cold it was. The maintenance man said there was no way to control the temperature in each room and that it was adjusted for the entire floor by one thermostat. That really freaked me out. Could it have been the medication, or was I really getting

Divine messages from the Holy Spirit?

That afternoon, I had a vision, and I wrote down names and instructions beside each name as they were given to me. Beside Andrea's name, I had written, "Flowers will grow where knives were sown." Two years later, when I was back at St Mike's for attempting suicide, I saw Andrea signing in to visit someone on the 17th floor. When I approached her, I saw that she had covered the tattoos of razor blades on her arms with images of flowers. The nurse, Tatiana, was on duty that day and she shared with Andrea what had happened years earlier. I would later learn that my doctors had considered me delusional for making these predictions, but after that day, they couldn't explain how the predictions came true.

Back in July 2009, what happened after supper was that I was told by God to go into the quiet room and sit beside Andrea and hold her hand. I went to the room and found her sitting on a yoga mat. I sat down beside her and asked if it was okay if I held her hand. She did not respond, but I took her hand in mine and was instantly aware of the hell that she was living through. I went through the bowels of hell with her, seeing the demons and horrors that she had lived through, and it made me sick. I soon let go of her hand and I was transported back into the room, feeling nauseous. I ran to the bathroom and threw up.

That wasn't the first time I was taken into someone else's hell and got violently sick; it had also happened years earlier. When

Father Yves, an elderly priest in our church, Immaculate Conception, heard bad confessions that upset him, he would come to me and let me be a kind of garbage truck to process what he had heard, and I would either throw up or get irritable bowel syndrome and flush out the sins through my body.

With Andrea, it was the exact same thing. Andrea's husband, Mike, stopped me one day in the hall and said, "I don't know what you're doing to my wife, but keep doing it. It's working." Months later, I would meet Andrea and Mike at a bar and find out that things had worked out. Andrea was coping really well, and they ended up buying me dinner that night.

Later that day, I received a message from God to wash Andrea's feet, so I set about getting a wash basin, some soap, and some towels. I washed Andrea's feet in the TV room, but she just stared off into nothing with no reaction. Later, my friend Tammy Moone came to visit me at the hospital and she brought her guitar. Tammy and I set up a little talent show in the TV room. Andrea was still sitting there as we started singing popular tunes but getting the words all wrong. It didn't take very long for us to be in tears from laughing as we regaled the other patients and nurses with a Wayne and Shuster-type sing-along. At one point, some police officers who were dropping off a new patient came into the room to see what all the noise was about and burst into laughter when they started hearing the lyrics that we were singing to popular songs. For the first time, I saw Andrea laugh and I knew that she was starting to become herself again. It turned out to be a wonderful evening and I slept without incident that night.

My good friend Tammy Moone playing her guitar and singing for us.

I was discharged after breakfast without any medication and with no place to go. As I reached the front door on Victoria Street, my entire body started to shake and despite being a mechanic, I found myself afraid of cars. My car wasn't where I had left it, so I called Maria, and she told me that my dad had taken it back with them when they had left the hospital a week earlier.

I was now stranded in Toronto. I called some friends to come and help me cross the street and they took me out for lunch. Later, we took a taxi to the apartment where I had been renting a room from a new acquaintance, only to find that the locks had been changed and I was told to go away. It turned out that Maria and my father had also gone there and convinced Brenda that it was not safe to have me living there. For the first time in my life, I found myself homeless and isolated with just a bag of clothes. After speaking to a friend, Shadmith, she advised me to try to go to the Gerstein Crisis Centre. I soon found myself in tears, knocking at their door in the middle of the night, looking for a bed to sleep in. Thus began my life as a homeless woman.

Another canary was lost in a coal mine.

The Rose

by Stefonknee Wolscht

In a field of green nestled on a country farm at the edge of a cold, hard concrete city, a single rose reaches towards the sky.

Escaping the frigid earth, she is caressed by the gentle breeze of an early morning spring day and finds warmth in the sun. Hidden in a field of green, she finds her place in the world.

Existing within a world seemingly oblivious to her, a world that she cannot comprehend or understand... nor does she wish to... she conforms.

She conforms as best she can and seeks to blend in to survive, her identity lost among the countless shades of green that stretch beyond the eye, where they meet a sky of blue.

But alas, she fails, for within the sea of greens, a rose must stand alone, rejected and hurt. She is dropped and trampled underfoot, lost but for a single seed.

A seed blown in a breeze and washed away finds a new home within a crack in the concrete sidewalk of a cold, hard city and is reborn.

Escaping the frigid earth, she is caressed by the gentle breeze of an early morning spring day and finds warmth in the sun. Hidden in a forgotten alley, she finds her place in the world.

She exists within a world evolving at the speed of light, seemingly oblivious to her, a world that she cannot comprehend or understand... nor does she wish to... she conforms.

She conforms as best she can and seeks to blend in to survive, her identity lost among the countless shades of grey that stretch beyond the eye, where they meet a sky of blue.

But alas, she is found, for within a sea of greys, a rose must stand alone, rescued and loved. She is transplanted and nurtured and encouraged to grow.

She blossoms and blooms into the beautiful rosebush she was meant to be, bringing colour and fragrance to a cold hard city.

She finds purpose in bringing joy to all but herself. She is unaware of her beauty and fragrance, she cannot see herself or understand her purpose, and she is alone.

A single rose reaches towards the sky, a sky of blue she knows too well. The morning dew weighs heavy on her heart and forms a tear that falls and is lost in a cold hard world.

Chapter 2
Dr. Kaz and my kids

At St Mike's, I met a therapist named Dr. Kaz, a middle-aged man with kind eyes and a gentle demeanour. I really liked him because he treated everyone with respect and dignity and took the time needed to understand and accept us as we were. Dr. Kaz wanted to talk to me about my children. In one of the sessions, we went back to when my first daughter was born and discussed what it was like to become a parent for the first time. Talking about my kids and the life I'd had, made me feel better. Somehow, getting the thoughts out of my head and hearing the words come out of my mouth made me feel like I was still part of my children's lives.

Dr. Kaz had an assistant, Barbara, who would do crafts and other activities like painting nails with us to help us pass the time. They worked well as a team, and I really liked her; she was pretty and very considerate to all the patients. She helped us to open up and talk about our feelings as we were distracted by doing stuff with our hands. This seemed to work well for me and helped me better understand what was happening to me mentally.

Maria and I had become pregnant in the fall of 1986, so that's where I began talking to Dr. Kaz about my children. Maria and I had often talked about having seven children in the five years we were dating, and we agreed that getting married and starting a family would be a good idea. By June 19, 1987, we were at the hospital awaiting the birth of our new baby. As it happened, on that day, we were at my parents' house dropping off stuff to put in their yard sale when Maria's water broke. We both were very nervous, not knowing what to expect or how long it would take for our newborn to arrive. I sped from my parents' farm to the hospital as fast as I could, to get there in time for the delivery.

As it turned out, it was a long labour with a lot of ups and downs. Eventually, we found ourselves in the delivery room, Maria screaming in pain with each contraction and me there with my left arm acting as the stirrups and my right arm under Maria's neck, cradling her head, because it was a busy night and there were no other delivery beds available. With her face to my face, nose to nose, we gave birth to a beautiful baby girl, Chavonne, on June 20.

My immediate reaction was *I love you*, and *Oh my God, I'm a parent. Now, what do I do?* I think that was the first time I fell in love in my entire life, in love with this little girl that we created. Right from the very first moment I saw her, I knew she was a miracle. She cried right away, healthy, strong, and loud, testing her new lungs. I knew at that moment that I could be a great mom because I loved her more than anything in the world. Tears filled my eyes as I carried her over to be cleaned off and weighed, and as I held her tight in my arms, my life had forever been changed. I was now responsible for another person's life.

I was still a kid, just twenty-three, but I loved introducing Chavonne as "my daughter" to visitors as they came to the hospital.

Chavonne was my parents' first grandchild and the second grandchild for Maria's parents, but the first female baby on both sides of the family. She was adored by all. Maria and I loved shopping for her, getting her stuffies and pretty little baby girl dresses. It was so nice to be able to go to stores and buy dresses in doll sizes. It made me feel like a real girl inside. Everywhere we went, people would tell us how beautiful she was. She was an instant sensation with her huge smile, blonde hair, and blue eyes. Chavonne was a great baby as far as sleeping and eating; she had a great appetite, and she was very healthy. There's something about the smell of a new baby that warms my heart and makes me love them even more. I believe they're a miracle sent by God to teach us the meaning of life.

Chavonne was a favourite of our neighbour Tina Kotov, an elderly Russian woman who lost her husband after World War II when he was sent to Siberia, never to return. Tina and Nick Kotov, her second husband, were the original owners of the piece of property that I'd bought to build my house on. They sold five one-acre parcels of land, zoned for single-family dwellings. I got the piece of land from my brother-in-law, Brad McCartney, who had an open mortgage with Nick and Tina, which was transferred to me. I was an apprentice mechanic earning good money, so I quadrupled the payments and managed to pay the land off in five years.

By the time Chavonne was two, I was building the house that would become our family home and Nick and Tina gave me a new mortgage to help finish the construction. Tina only had one son, Bobby, then in his sixties, who was still single, having never married, and still tied to her apron strings. Tina was hoping Bobby would give her grandchildren; a baby girl like Chavonne was exactly what Tina needed to fulfill her life. She would babysit more often than we needed her, and she would spoil Chavonne more than my own parents would. My parents loved Chavonne, of course, but they also loved their retirement and travelling in their motor home. They preferred to come and visit us and then be on their way.

Nick and Tina were like grandparents to me. We weren't just neighbours; we were really good friends too. They've since passed on, and I really miss sitting in their backyard with the kids, drinking lemonade on hot summer days.

The year after Chavonne was born, we found ourselves back in the delivery room on July 21, 1988, when we delivered our second daughter, a beautiful little girl we named Amanda. With her brunette hair and huge brown eyes, you'd never have guessed that she was Chavonne's sister. And being the second child, she didn't get the attention that Chavonne got when she was born. While she and her mother were in the hospital, I was so busy taking care of our first baby that I even forgot to print a birth announcement. By that time, I was not only a full-time mechanic, but I was also busy building our house anytime I could and still delivering newspapers at night. I juggled all that and raising two little girls while Maria attended school. This left my brain a little frazzled as to what details needed to be covered.

I had fallen in love with beautiful little Amanda from the moment she was born, and we bonded right away. Amanda wasn't as easy to take care of in the beginning as Chavonne had been. Unlike her sister, she cried a lot at night, so to give Maria and Chavonne a break, I would take Amanda with me at one a.m. when I left to deliver newspapers. She would sleep fine listening to the radio and the purr of the engine. When she was awake, I would sing along with the radio to make her smile. We had a lot of time together to create a powerful bond.

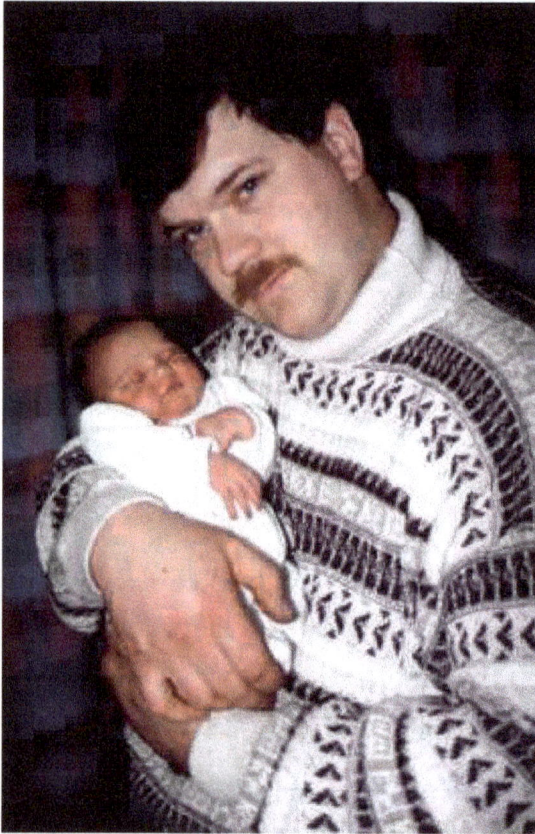

Amanda and Daddy (July 1988)

Maria's parents simply adored grandchildren. Grandma and Grandpa went out of their way to gather up all their grandchildren so that the cousins could spend a lot of time playing together at their house. Grandma was a teacher and would come and pick up all her grandchildren from each family a couple times a week when she wasn't working. Especially during her summer vacation, she'd take them home with her to spoil them with Italian cooking. This proved very helpful because it allowed me to focus on my work when all the babies were with their grandma and grandpa. Our children bonded really well with their cousins, and I'm happy to say that all of the cousins are best friends to this day.

The Wolscht Family Reunion at the 11A Farm (2009)

During this time, Maria was still a student at York University. During the day, it was very common for me to have the two little babies out in the shop while I was fixing cars. They would be in a high chair eating and playing or asleep in their playpen.

When I wasn't fixing cars, I'd spend hours playing with our kids in the house. I learned something valuable from my father-in-law, Rocco. He taught me to get down and lie on the floor so I would be at their level. I would just lie there and let them play while I played along. Playing with toddlers and changing diapers was very uncommon for men at that time. The only way my dad would change a diaper was to have the kids strip down on the front lawn and wash them off with a garden hose from twenty feet away. I enjoyed being a mom to them, so changing diapers was just part of the job. Don't get me wrong: diapers really stink, and babies fill them up quickly, but dressing them up and putting on the new diaper was like being a girl with dolls playing mommy, which was something I was never allowed to do as a child.

Having children was amazing; their kindness and love made the world a better place. We had our two little girls, and then in September 1989, we had a miscarriage, which left us heartbroken. We worried that it was our fault for getting pregnant too soon. It's very hard to be a good parent when everything's going well, but it's even harder once you lose a child. It took us a while to trust ourselves again, but two years later, on December 21, 1991, we had our first little boy, Christopher, which helped us emotionally. Things started to feel normal again, and we looked like a nice little Catholic family. Christopher was a very happy baby, always smiling and oh so kind, even as a young child. He was a little angel and he would even offer his bottle to other babies if they were crying. We were extremely lucky to have such lovely children.

I may have stretched myself too thin between raising our kids and working all my jobs. I was totally exhausted, and by the summer of 1992, I took to my bed running a fever for several days and my hearing became super sensitive. If someone was walking around the house, it sounded like thunder. I ended up getting an appointment to see our family doctor. She checked me over and stated that it was unusual for someone to have a fever at my age, so she asked that I go to Emerg to have it checked out. Before leaving, she assured me that it should be something simple and nothing complicated like meningitis. I was in Emerg for eight hours, lying on a gurney in the hall with no protection for the other patients around me. After doing a spinal tap, the emergency room physicians came to my bed, covered head to toe in hazmat suits. I was transferred up to the palliative care unit of York Region Hospital with meningitis, one of the most painful things that I've ever experienced. The pain in my spine was so intense that I couldn't feel my neck or head anymore. I was kept isolated in palliative care while they tried to figure out what kind of meningitis it was.

The day after I was admitted, the nurses told me that Dr. Merrow was in the hospital and would come to see me that day. I asked them if they could put a toe tag on my toe as a joke about her diagnosis of its not being meningitis. The nurse assured me that they couldn't do that, but they would let my doctor know that I was still functioning well enough to play along with a joke. I think I had taken on too much and now my body was sending me a message, telling me to slow down.

There were three other meningitis patients in Ontario that summer, two men from Carleton University in Ottawa and a woman in Orangeville. Unfortunately, the three of them passed away. This news caused me to worry about who would provide for my young family if I died, too. As it turned out, by the grace of God, I was lucky enough to survive. I remained isolated in palliative care for weeks.

I remember my parents coming to check in on me. My mother asked if there was something they could do to help. I asked if they would get some milk and diapers for the babies.

My father said, "No, you are an adult. You need to take care of your family yourself." I never forgave my father for this. My mother wanted to help but he refused to give in at a time when I needed my parents the most.

After leaving the hospital, I spent the next three months recuperating in my bed because of a pinched nerve at T-4 in my spine. With Maria still in university, we racked up bills and fell behind in our payments. Eventually, we had to extend our mortgage, and the debt survived longer than our marriage.

After Christopher, we welcomed our fourth child and second son, Michael, on June 5, 1993. He was a very active baby with an abundance of energy, keeping us on our toes. Michael always found ways to get into mischief, but he finally relaxed once we gave him paper and a pencil to draw, which helped calm him down. He's the artist in our family. Michael had a mischievous look in his eyes whenever he felt like doing something funny, and we quickly learned that he expressed his love by doing silly things. I loved them all for being who they were, each of our children for being so unique, yet they all bonded with each other.

With her big green/grey/blue eyes that forever changed like a mood ring, Nicole was born on February 14, 1996, our Valentine's baby. Maria had been at Chavonne and Amanda's school that day, helping organize a Valentine's dance. I remember she came home and very calmly announced to me, while I was fixing a car in the garage, that the baby was coming, but to finish my work and not to worry while she'd packed a bag for the hospital. I couldn't believe how calm we had become about childbirth by the time Nicole came along. It seemed as if it was just another thing to schedule for that day. Nicole was baby number five, so I gave her the nickname "Nickel." She was very playful and was like a doll to her older sisters, who, by this time, were helping us raise "the babies."

After Nicole came our third son, Peter, on June 10, 1997. He was a preemie who came into the world at only 3lbs 8oz, no bigger than a squirrel. He fit in the palm of my hand. We visited him in his incubator for several weeks before welcoming him home to meet the crowd. Peter was our miracle baby, and somehow, he survived despite tying his umbilical cord into knots while he swam around in his mother's womb. But he did survive and was very healthy, although we as parents had to prove to CAS that we were capable of taking care of such a small child, despite having five other children. As a young child, Peter was a joker and loved to keep us laughing.

Finally, our seventh and last child, Robert, was born on December 20, 1998. He was a lighthearted little guy who stole our hearts with his smile and his laughter. It wouldn't take very long before Robert was the same size as Peter, which pleased Maria because she'd always wanted to have twins. Having two sons the same size allowed her to raise them like twins, and they are still best friends. In our family, Robert, Peter, and Nicole were known as "the babies."

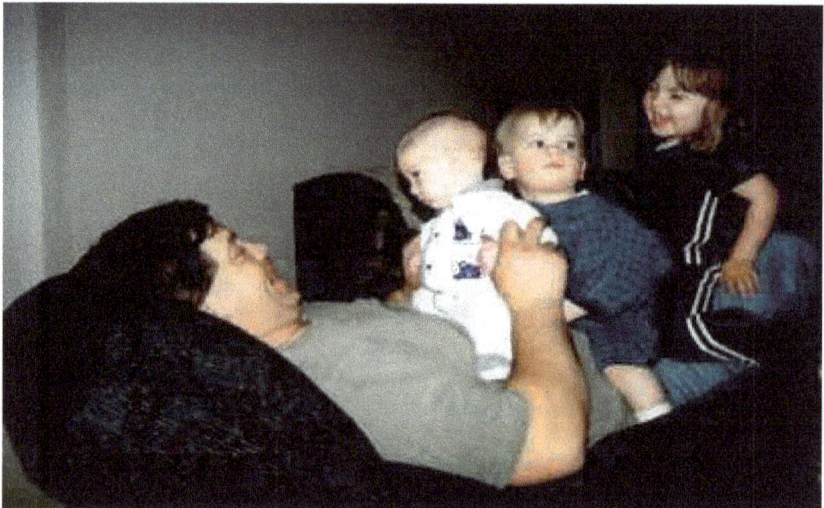

Daddy with Robert, Peter and Nicole (November 1999)

At this point, we definitely looked like your average Catholic family. All the kids were special and each one was unique in their own way. All the while, in my own mind, I was enjoying being a mom to the seven little miracles. I created a math word problem after Robert was born: when someone asked how many kids we had, I would say, "My daughter has twice as many brothers as sisters, and my son has the same number of brothers as sisters, you do the math!" We had a perfect family and they all got along really well. By this time, our house was finished and my shop set up, so I no longer need to deliver newspapers at night.

Can you see how I'm still doing it? Saying less and less about each child because we got busier and busier with each baby, and they all merged into one cohesive group we called "The Wolscht Kids."

I told Dr. Kaz that having children was the best thing I did with my life and that my children filled my heart with love and gave my life purpose until suddenly they were gone. The kids would be with me every day while I ran my business from home and Maria went off to work as a French teacher at Pickering College. Those were the best fifteen years of my life, but one by one, they would be old enough to get on the school bus and head off to school. It was hard for me watching them grow up and now I realize that I was codependent with my kids. My pride and pleasure in them gave me all my happiness… I had totally fallen in love with each one of them.

Daddy praying the Rosary with Peter and Nicole (Easter 2002)

No doubt they were amazing kids, talented, smart and kind. Whether it was music, sports, or academics, they all seemed to thrive at anything they tried. I remember once, when Christopher was about five years old, I decided to take him by bus and subway to Maple Leaf Gardens in Toronto, an hour away, for his first hockey game. On the subway, Christopher befriended a homeless man. He sat down beside him and asked the man if he was going to see the hockey game too, then went on to regale him with our itinerary for the evening. Chris was so excited. Everyone in our subway car was listening intensely to this little kid telling the world about his adventure. Here was this child teaching us to accept everyone as equals; he did not judge this man for being homeless. Before we got off the subway I noticed a few moist eyes. Christopher could naturally reach past barriers to unite people and spread unconditional love. He continues to naturally reunite people to this day.

Wolscht kids building a "Quinzee"

In August 2004, I injured my left leg, it got infected, and gangrene set in. At the hospital, the doctors circled the black spot on my leg below my left knee and put me on an infusion pump to administer antibiotics. The following day, the black spot had grown considerably larger, so they punctured my skin with needles and started squeezing out old blood. At home that night, my eight-year-old daughter, Nicole, heard what they had done and started doing the same for me, squeezing dark, smelly blood into a bucket for a couple of hours. The next day, the doctors were surprised to see the positive results. They thought they'd need to amputate my leg to save my knee. Nurses came to our house each day for the next while to replace the hoses and change the dressing. Having heard what Nicole had done for me, they had her change hoses and dressings on her teddy bear. Nicole saved my left leg, and I will forever be grateful to her for that.

I remember often playing silly games with the kids. At Christmas time, when unwrapping our presents, it was a tradition for us to take the wrapping paper and make paper snowballs and have a snowball fight in the living room around the Christmas tree. Often, we made snow angels with them in the backyard in freshly fallen snow. Whether bantering around the dining room table about the day's events over dinner, or spending one on one time doing the dishes, we would always share our days' events and our bond would grow stronger. I still look back at all of it fondly.

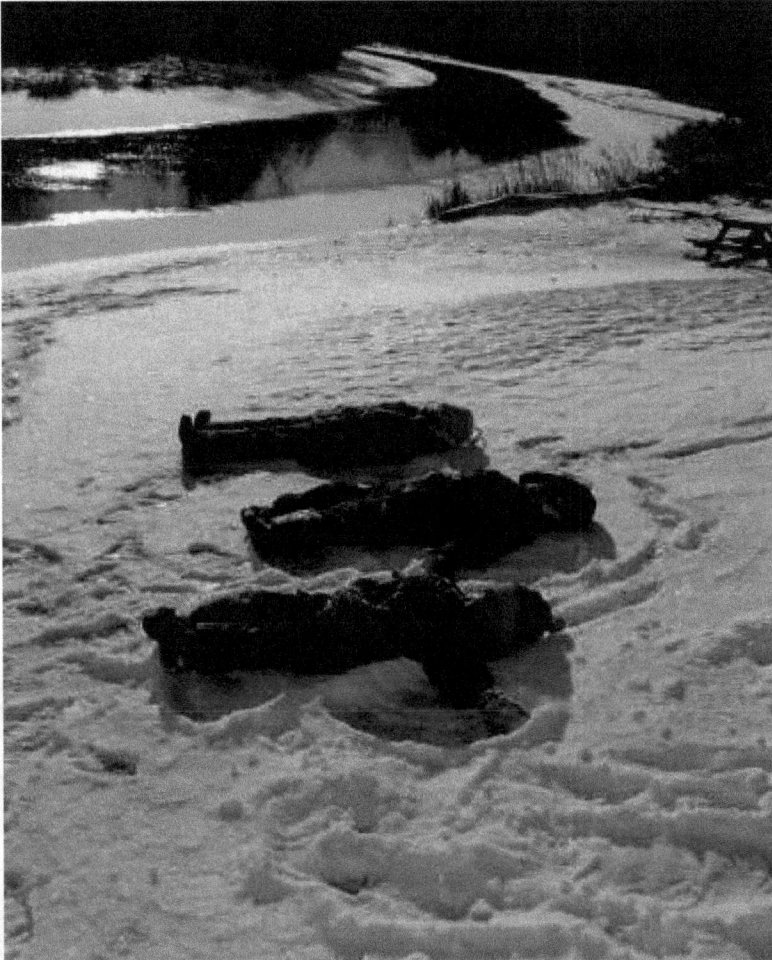

Our children making snow angels in our backyard (January 2001)

Many school mornings, to speed up breakfast, I would sing them a little song I made up, and it went like this... "I love peanut butter; I love fresh bread too. When you spread peanut butter on my bread, I chew, chew, chew, chew, chew. Yum!" On "yum," they would all take another bite of their sandwich. We would eat and dance into each new day.

Another thing I loved to do when sending them off to school was to tell them, "Don't learn too much today. Save some for tomorrow." But on Fridays, I would say, "Learn as much as you can today… there's no school tomorrow." Having kids was the best thing that ever happened to me. I highly recommend starting a family to anyone who's looking for true love.

My kids all enjoyed skating lessons, and we enjoyed being at the arena, meeting other skating families and watching them grow stronger and stronger. They got so excited when they were part of a team and were able to master new skills.

Our kids participating at Stars on Ice

What really stirred them up was when the Canadian women's hockey team won a gold medal. The Canadian women's team beat the odds; while being shorthanded most of the game to the American team they still took the gold with a 2-0 win. Immediately after that, my two oldest girls wanted to switch from figure skating to hockey. Chavonne played goalie and Amanda played right wing. We would all listen intently as Amanda played because when she took the puck off someone, she would always say, "I'm sorry," and continue on. She apologized loud enough that everyone in the arena could hear it. She was too cute.

Chavonne (pink bandana) with "Sutton Sabres" girls hockey team.

There are too many stories to put into one book but suffice it to say we had a lot of fun. We also worked hard. The kids had chores to do in the house, and we would spend winter weekends at my family's farm, cutting firewood to heat the house. One time, when my leg was broken, we had skids delivered by the truckload to our house to cut up for the fireplaces. The older kids would rip the skids apart, I would cut the pieces on an old table saw, and then Maria and the little kids would pile up the wood.

***

Doctor Kaz tried unsuccessfully to get Maria to bring the children down to see him so he could get to know them, hear their side of the story, and eventually start group therapy for all of our benefits. Maria would have no part of it. She was determined to keep me separated from the kids as much as possible. This made me really hate her, and I wondered why my being transgender was enough of a reason to break up our happy family.

Clockwise from left: Nicole, Robert, Amanda, Chris, Michael, Dad and Peter at Octoberfest 2002

Having the kids back in my life would have been the best medicine for my depression but it wasn't to be. I would later realize that Maria was manipulating a lot of family and friends by controlling the narrative in my absence. She would threaten to exclude people from seeing our kids if they talked to me or visited me in the shelter. I'm not sure what she told our children, but she had studied child psychology in school and knew enough to make them hate me and be afraid of me. I think that this kind of manipulation is commonly referred to as Parental Alienation Syndrome (P.A.S.)

I would later find out that the priest from our parish believed that I was "possessed by the Evil One" for being transgender. I know that a lot of people think that I'm a bad person for leaving her and the kids, but I really could not stop being transgender. I really wanted us all to get back together again and work things out, but I soon realized that it would be impossible to resurrect the life we once had.

I carry a lot of guilt for being born into this body, but during that time, no one could have hated me more than I hated myself. The stigma and hate for trans people aren't only directed at the individual; it also stigmatizes our parents, siblings, spouses, and children. Transphobia hurts everyone.

Annual skiing trips to Horseshoe Valley (March 2001)

I struggled with my Catholic religion, my faith, and my relationship with God because of being born transgender; I can only imagine how it affected my family and friends. It often feels like a cruel joke that is perpetuated by religions and ignorant people. My prayer would often be, "God, you promised not to give me a cross that was too heavy to bear... You lied."

Anyway, let's get back to my visits with Dr. Kaz. He was amazing at helping me understand my mental health issues. He would compare me to a hunted rabbit who never knew when it would be safe to raise her head out of the ground. He would say that the vagus nerve, the oldest nerve in the body of mammals, is responsible for our Fight, Flight, or Freeze reaction. When we are hunted or the nerve is overstimulated, we begin to panic, and this constant suffering can lead to Complex PTSD. Unlike simple PTSD, which occurs after a traumatic episode is over, complex PTSD is ongoing, and we are never really separated from our triggers. A soldier returning from war cannot leave the war behind despite being safe at home again. Complex PTSD is remaining in the "war zone" with no escape. Our vagus nerve remains overstimulated, causing anxiety to be continually triggered and often leaving us depressed.

I would meet Dr. Kaz a lot over the next fourteen years, and he did a lot to help me through those dark and difficult days. I feel like I don't thank him enough for saving my life, but he provided me with some of the best therapy that I got during my depression.

You Are Loved
by Stefonknee Wolscht

You walked through life with me, and we laughed, cried, cheered. We were brave together and we trembled in fear.

Together, we stepped along the path that had been our life. Like stones in the rushing river, we navigated our way along. We chose each step as best we could with the information and strength we possessed at that time.

Holding On by a Thread

We survived! We remember, looking back, we laughed, and we cried. It is what it is. No more, no less, my life.

At times, I loved you, but at times I hated you. Not because of who you are but because we were taught that you were less. You believed what others said because they controlled your perception of what you were, what you were to be, and what you could never achieve.

Put aside all of these "rules." Come with me and let's go skip from stone to stone, hand in hand, through life and what it may hold. I can't promise you sunny days or calm seas. What I can promise is, I will never harm you or leave you in darkness.

We are moving forward because we cannot go back. What's done is done. Let us learn from our adventures and let us be inspired to be all we can be. We will still be laughed at and ridiculed, but we know that what we cannot hide lives in everyone around us, very deep in their soul. We reflect a truth that they may not comprehend. A truth that they cannot accept.

A truth that we are a creation loved by our creator and created in love.

We are loved, if only by our creator.

We can take that love and share it with others so that they may know that they are loved, too.

We have all been hurt by someone, and we have all hurt someone.

Move forward now and embrace life as a loved creation that has the gift to say, "I LOVE YOU!"

I love you in times of fear and isolation.

I love you when you are sad and need to cry.

I love you when times are good and we are surrounded by friends.

But I love you most when we leap towards a stone that seems too far to reach and splash into the water, content in knowing we gave it our best, and we laughed as we leaped into the unknown.

I LOVE YOU

Chapter 3
The Gerstein/ Women's Res/ Arrest #1

After leaving St. Mike's on August 6, 2009, I ended up at the Gerstein Crisis Centre. I had never been without a home before in my life, and this felt really weird.

That July, I had begun the process of establishing myself in the city. I'd wanted to open a lesbian bar in Toronto, so I teamed up with my friend Arden Ruttan to start that business together. It was a dream and a mission for me, to create a place where lesbians and trans women could dance and socialize safely. We finally found a property for sale that was perfect for our needs. We were in the process of closing the deal to buy 781 Queen Street East when everything went wrong. I had already put $40,000 down as a deposit on the deal, plus Arden came up with $10,000. We each would need to invest $91,000 and the bank had approved us for a mortgage for the balance of the $705,000. I needed another $51,000 to finalize the deal that was due to close on July 31.

781 Queen Street East Toronto, Ontario (July 2009)

Feeling desperate, I had asked my wife if she would borrow that amount from my father, as he wouldn't talk to me (because I was transgender) and, in return, she could keep both our homes and all our assets. My father lent her the money, but Maria would not release the funds unless I signed a separation agreement that included my not wearing women's clothes or appearing in public as a woman.

I just couldn't do it; I had been living with that lie for too long already. I panicked and thought all was lost. A lawyer friend advised me not to sign the deal because if I agreed to "not present as female," I would be signing away my human rights. So, there I was, on July 23, one week from the closing date, without any means to close the deal. In a panic and full of despair, I decided to commit suicide so that my life insurance would pay for the building.

We both fell short of the balance owing as Arden had not told his wife, Anne, and she did not support the idea of us running a lesbian bar. All these problems put my life into a tailspin. Now homeless and alone in a crisis centre, crying and shaking, I knew I was experiencing a mental meltdown. Anxiety, depression, and PTSD all rolled into one big breakdown.

Scared as I was that first week at the crisis centre, I did manage to get out of the real estate deal. The owners quickly relisted the property and sold it for more than what we had committed to. One crisis was resolved, but I was still here in Toronto, with no car, no money, no place to live, and no access to my children. I was extremely anxious, not knowing how long I could stay at the crisis center, and not knowing how I would fit into society. Things were happening around me and to me that I had no control over, and this was completely foreign to someone who had so much in my previous life.

At the crisis centre, they make life very simple for the clients. When you wake up in the morning, you just make your bed and come downstairs, and coffee is already made. You help yourself to whatever you feel like eating for breakfast as they have a huge pantry and a big walk-in cooler with everything you could imagine. I think when people are in crisis, they eat more, or maybe they use eating as a way to cope with their crisis. Either way, meals and snacks are essential and at the Gerstein, they had very healthy food, with lots of fruit and vegetables. We would just help ourselves to leftovers from the previous evening or make our own meal for lunch. After lunch, the staff would start cooking a beautiful meal that we would eat together as one cohesive group at the big dining room table. Throughout the day, we got to know each other as we did some art therapy. In my case, I worked with a social worker on resolving my real estate deal. Every shift change, a worker would come and ask me how I was getting along and if I was comfortable. They were very concerned about everyone's well-being. I wish I could have stayed there longer but they needed beds for other people in crisis and so I was eventually transferred out.

After ten days at the Gerstein, my crisis worker found a bed for me in a local women's shelter at Dundas Street and Bathurst called Women's Residence. I had never been homeless and penniless, isolated from family and friends before, and this was a frightening step. I found myself moving into a building where their biggest concern was making sure I wasn't bringing in bedbugs. I didn't even know what a bedbug was. Here, I was sharing a room with five other marginalized women who were complete strangers.

Holding On by a Thread

I didn't know how to be homeless—I had no idea that there were options for me, nor could I comprehend how to get some kind of income to ever get out of this situation. I didn't realize it at the time, but it would have been nice to have somebody who could help me navigate my way through the system and tell me what to expect along the way.

Living in a shelter isn't easy under the best circumstances, but having so many people dealing with addictions and their individual crises in one place made it very difficult to be supportive of each other. Besides sharing a room with five complete strangers, all dealing with their own issues and struggles, I was expected to abide by all the rules. For example, constantly stripping down the bed and laundering all your clothes and bedding to avoid bedbugs. A frustrating thing in the shelter was having only one TV and the remote for only one hour in the communal television room—after each hour, you had to walk down four flights of stairs to return the remote just so someone else could take the remote back up the four flights of stairs to keep the TV on. Watching TV, going for walks, or crying in my bed seemed to be the only activities available to me there. Eventually I would find out that there were rooms in the basement where they would help us prepare ourselves for the job market by writing resumes and improving our computer skills.

The rules were also applied in the dining hall, and I remember always feeling weak and hungry. I was weak probably because of everything that was happening to my body or maybe it was the medication I was on, and I was also hungry because the portions were too small for me. I'm a 6'2, 260 lbs trans woman. I need more food than your average cisgender woman, but in a shelter, you can't ask for seconds. You can't even ask people for the food that they're about to throw out because it could be interpreted as a form of bullying, so during my short stay at Women's Residence, I lost twenty-five pounds.

I was a complete mess and after a week of crying, I decided to go to the public library across the street to check out a book. I figured reading would be a good way to distract me and pass the time. I was searching on the computer for a good book to take out when I got a phone call from York Regional Police telling me that they had a warrant for my arrest. I gathered up my stuff and went back to the shelter, again shaking and crying, completely scared and confused. What could I have done to have the police want to arrest me? I didn't see myself as one of "those" people. The police used to be my friends.

I talked to my social worker, who gave me the phone number of a lawyer, which I copied onto my arm with a marker. I then called our parish priest, Fr. Herman Dias, who I thought was my friend, and asked him if he could come down and pick me up so I could turn myself in at 3 District in Sutton. It was late when Father Herman got to Toronto, and I had been pacing the floor both inside the shelter and outside on the sidewalk since one p.m. It was well past seven, and I was frustrated and afraid. I worried that the police would be upset with me because it was really dark by the time we got to the police station. Fr. Herman offered to hold on to my phone, locker key, and purse so that I wouldn't lose them while in jail.

I went inside and spoke to the front desk clerk, who then took me to the back, where they processed me and put me into a cell. I asked if I could call a lawyer, but they said they would take the number and call her for me. There I was with nothing else to do other than to follow an officer to my cell. Once I got into the cell, I couldn't sit on the concrete bed because the heater underneath made it way too hot. I sat on the floor. I was shaking and crying, my heart hurt, and I was so afraid. What was happening? My life was turned upside down and I was in jail. And for what? *What did I do? Why did they arrest me?* The police wouldn't tell me anything.

No information, no questioning, just me there alone in a concrete cell with the light on all night. I was completely confused. What happened to all the police friends that I had in York Region who came to my shop to have their cars fixed? Where were they now, and why weren't they speaking up for me? Where were all these friends now that I needed them, now that I was alone and being hunted? Where were they?

Time seems to go by much slower when you're locked up in a cell without a window or clock. I had no way of knowing what would happen next, so I waited and waited. After some time, a three-legged cricket came under the door and hopped in circles in my cell. I lay down to block the crack under the door so that he couldn't get out and we kept each other company for the night. I worried that if he was found in the hall, they might step on him and kill him, so I spent the night telling him about everything that was happening to me.

The next morning, an officer offered to get me food, but I declined the gesture. A cop friend of mine had once confided in me that officers often spit in prisoners' food—so much for innocent until proven guilty. My heart was still racing, and my chest hurt; my arms and legs tingled. I still had no idea why I had been arrested, and I hadn't heard anything about them contacting my lawyer, so I was a mess. Before long, I was processed and ushered into a transport van with other prisoners, each in their own metal cell, heading to the courthouse in Newmarket.

Shackled and handcuffed, I was being bounced around in my cell inside the transport van like a pinball. There was no place to sit, and the steel floor was too hot to lie down on. They seemed to be driving extra fast and braking extra hard. I ended up lodging myself into the step by the door to keep from injuring myself.

Once we got to the courthouse, I was ushered into another small cell and offered some water and a sandwich. I was not hungry, so I refused their offer. The prisoner in the cell to my right had kicked the van on his way out, so the police refused to take off his handcuffs, which are very painful, to punish him. I lay down in that cell all day long, staring at the ceiling. Finally, I was transferred to a different cell to see a judge on a television screen and speak into a microphone. I still had no idea why I had been arrested or what I was being charged with. Also, I couldn't see what was happening on the television screen because tears constantly filled my eyes. During the interview, no one was talking to me. I was there but I was invisible, although they seemed to be talking about me in the courtroom. The legal system is not what you see on TV. It's a lot of finger-pointing and accusations with no evidence or crime scene. They were accusing me of assaults, uttering threats, destruction of private property, and a dozen other charges that were thrown out before I was arrested. I felt like I was dying, and no one cared. I was a prisoner in a system that treated you like you're guilty from the moment they put handcuffs on you. Sometime later, perhaps six or seven p.m., I was released from jail and told that I was not to return to York Region except for court appointments. My first appointment would be the next morning to sign the papers for my release because, by that time, the offices were closed for the day.

Outside the courthouse, I realized I had no phone, no keys, and no purse. They were still with Fr. Herman, wherever he was. I had no way to get out of York Region, so I had to hop onto a Viva bus without a pass. The irony did not escape me that, for the first time, I was breaking the law in order to abide by the court's ruling. I couldn't win. Either way, I would become a criminal. Once I was out of York Region, at the Finch subway station, still in tears, I told the ticket clerk that I didn't have any money, that I'd just been released from jail and had no way to get back down to Toronto. I had a piece of paper that stated I should be allowed to get on public transit for free, but he told me it was worthless, so I had to jump the turnstile. He didn't follow me. I ended up crying on the subway all the way back to the homeless shelter. I didn't care who was there to see me. I didn't care that I was crying in front of strangers all the way back to Toronto.

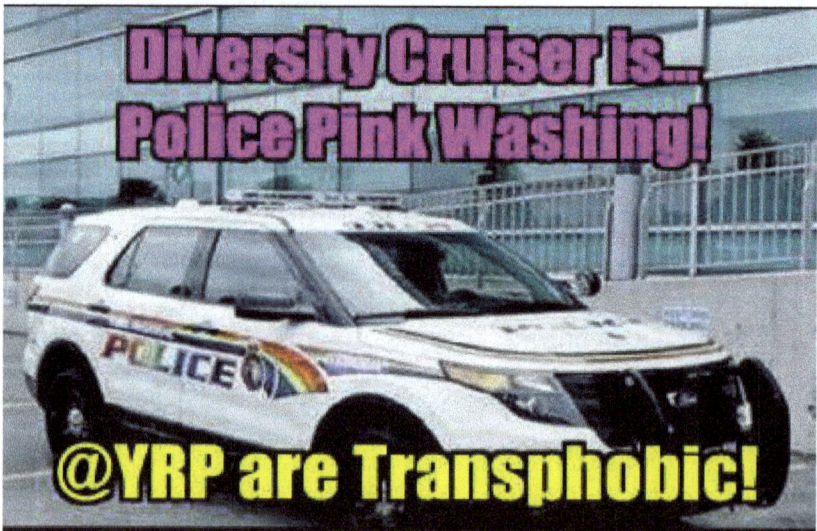

I would post this meme of the York Regional Police "Diversity Cruiser" on Twitter after their treatment of Transgender people like me!

Once back at the shelter one of the staff took me into a room to discuss what had happened and take notes for my file. I shared all I could remember and then went up to my bed around ten or eleven p.m. I was exhausted but couldn't sleep. My heart was racing and at two a.m. I walked across the street to Toronto Western Hospital. I had goosebumps on my arms, the hair on the back of my neck was standing straight, and my nerves were twitching under my skin all over my body. It looked as though spiders were crawling under my skin.

I was really sick. My heart hurt and I felt like I couldn't breathe. I went into Emerg, where I met a doctor who listened closely as I recounted what had transpired that day. He soon sedated me, and I fell asleep.

I woke up as some interns were making their morning rounds. They talked with me about my nervous system's reaction to what had happened the previous day. I was discharged but not before getting a note from the doctor with instructions for the police to bring me to the hospital rather than a police station if they were ever to arrest me again. I was told that doctors trump police. That was comforting to hear, and it helped alleviate some of the stress that I was feeling.

Back at the homeless shelter, the staff gave me $20 so I could get back up to Newmarket to sign the papers for my release they had issued the day before. Now, I would take the long, three-hour subway and bus ride to and from Newmarket courthouse, a trip I would make many times over the next six years.

Thankfully, I was assisted at the courthouse by an elderly white-haired woman, Beverly Snow, who carefully explained everything about my arrest and the conditions of my bail. She was very kind and treated me with respect. I discovered that my lawyer was never called, and that I was on my own to defend myself. I also found out that I would not get any documentation regarding the charges. Instead, it would be sent to Joanne Prince, the lawyer who was never contacted, the lawyer I couldn't have represented me because I didn't qualify for a legal aid certificate due to lack of evidence. I would later take a bus in the north end of the city to go and get my paperwork from her office so I could start to try to defend myself. I really hated what they were doing to me and how they were using the legal system to hurt me.

One of the conditions of my bail was that I had to visit the bail office at Old City Hall in Toronto twice a week to check in with a bail officer who would always misgender me. I was humiliated every time I went in to see her, first for having to wait in the hall dressed as a woman with hardened criminals, then in the bail office by this woman who took pleasure in insulting me because of my depression and gender expression.

A few weeks later, I learned in court that my wife had never called the police. Instead, that retired police officer from my church,

Rick Tracey, and his friends had called her and asked her to come into the local station to sign some papers to get me arrested. She had told the judge that I had never threatened her, yet the charges ranged from uttering threats to destruction of private property to assault and a dozen other charges, but I don't remember them all as they were thrown out before we went to trial. It seemed that my being "possessed by the Evil One" had trickled down to the congregation and these police officers took it upon themselves to make my life unbearable. Not only was I on trial for these criminal charges at that time, but I was also in family law court to decide the conditions of our separation and divorce. It would be an understatement to say I was overwhelmed by everything they were throwing at me. I felt defeated and alone. I could hardly stay awake on the bus ride up to the courthouse because of my medication, and during the trial, I would often fall asleep and not know what had transpired that day.

Twice, while at the court in Newmarket, I left the courthouse to go outside and attempt to take my own life. On one occasion, I overdosed on medication, and on another occasion, I broke the glass in my makeup mirror and used the broken glass to cut my wrists. Neither attempt was successful, and I just ended up back in the hospital.

Desperate and alone, I found myself more isolated than ever. I really missed my kids, and now it looked as though I would never see them again. Not only did Maria hate me, but it also seemed as though the whole system hated who I was and what I stood for. I really began to understand what discrimination looks and feels like. I had no way to contact my children and no way to know what they were thinking or how they were coping, and that broke my heart.

After the first criminal hearing, I was told to return back to Justice William Gorewich at a later date. He mentioned that he could see what was going on and wanted the trial to continue in his court. I felt like he was empathetic to me as a trans woman, only to find out the next time I came to court that my trial had been moved to a new judge, Justice Tetley. After many court dates and moving from one judge to another, without a lawyer and heavily sedated, I was completely overwhelmed by the whole ordeal. The entire process was confusing, and I didn't understand what was happening or how things would get resolved. At one point, they wouldn't even talk to me when it came to issues about my children, and instead, they had an alcoholic lawyer act as liaison between my children and the court. This guy was a complete fool: he couldn't remember the questions the court had asked him to ask my children, and things went out of control because he was an absolute drunk. He was just a waste of time. The whole ordeal looked hopeless.

Once while in the courthouse Beverly Snow overheard my father misgendering me and insulting me. She called him into her office and began lecturing him, she said that he was the same age as her and that he needed to get with the times and respect my gender identity. It felt good to hear somebody come to my defense.

Finally, on July 16, 2010, I was found guilty of assault and uttering threats. I was relieved that the trial was finally over, and I could go back to just being a homeless person. The so-called assault happened when we were cleaning up some junk in the garage and I tossed a small box of Beanie Babies to my wife that landed at her feet. The uttering threats occurred when, in desperation, I left a note on our front door stating that if Maria was going to separate me from our kids, I would fight her in court and she'd end up with nothing, and if there was anything left, I would burn it. She didn't keep the note, as she didn't take it as a real threat, but I told the judge that I had written it while feeling hopeless, pinned it to the front door, and returned to Toronto.

I got a conditional discharge when I appeared before the judge, finally, with a pro bono lawyer, Edward Prutschi, who empathized with me. He told the court that anything more than a conditional discharge and he would appeal the decision and get it thrown out. The conditions stated that I needed to stay out of York Region for the next two years, and to meet with a probation officer, Joanne Austin, to report what I had done each week. When I met with Joanne, I asked her if she would teach me to be a better person; she said maybe I was there to teach her. I thought, *great, the teacher is forced to be there for free and the student is getting paid. On what planet is that normal?*

I was also connected with a counselor at Sherbourne Health Center during this time. Her name was Carol Baker, and I spent many hours in her office and in group therapy, crying. She never judged me for being weak or being a trans woman, and I was always encouraged to share and participate. I remember one time calling her on my way home from family court to tell her I couldn't join the group therapy because I couldn't stop crying and I felt like I was ready to go to the hospital. Carol told me that this was the most important time for me to come. I didn't need to participate, just to be there and sit, watch, and listen as others did the activities. She said this would be enough to get me into a safe place. I took her advice and showed up for the session, where I sat in the corner, watching everyone do some therapeutic art. After a while, I stopped crying, and I realized it was the best thing for me to be among friends in a caring environment.

Stefonknee Wolscht and Carol Baker at Sherbourne Health (2009)

Test results from my hospital visit on September 4 indicated that I had suffered a minor heart attack when I was in jail and damaged a left valve in my heart. Needless to say, by this time, I had tried numerous times to end my life, but they hadn't worked. Being isolated and feeling hopeless was more than I could handle; being homeless, depressed, and a criminal made me ashamed of my life, not to mention the fact that I was a transgender woman separated from her children. Everything seemed overwhelming. This was all so new to me, and I couldn't believe that this was what my life had ended up like.

Just to make things worse, I was also suffering a bad reaction to Metformin. I had been diagnosed with prediabetes and the Metformin gave me diarrhea, which meant I had to stay close to a bathroom, although I also had to travel a lot by public transit. The medication wasn't doing anything to keep my glucose levels under control anyway, and my A1C was up in the mid-20s all the time.

In family court, Justice Ronald Kaufman said to my wife that not only was she a school principal, but she was also a full-time mother, raising seven children as he looked at me with disgust. I stood there in a dress with no way to explain to him that I had been the one raising our children—I was their mom, working three jobs so that she could got to school to be a school principal. I suspect Justice Kaufman may have had a connection to Pickering College, where Maria was director of the lower school.

To make everything worse, I was later arrested for not having my cell phone on my person or keeping my address at Women's Residence. I was taken down by two undercover police officers from York Region at a crosswalk in Toronto. The truth was that I had permission from the Newmarket and Toronto bail authorities to move from Women's Residence to a new shelter in central Toronto called Street Haven, and I had the documentation to prove it, only I had no way to get to the shelter to get it. They had also said that I didn't have my cell phone on, when in reality, it was in my pocket, and it was on. The police officers lied and told me that they had spent a week looking for me when all they needed to do was call me.

As I was being arrested on Pembroke Street, one of the managers of the shelter came running up and told the police officers that she had the documents on file and that they were not to arrest me but to take me to the hospital. She produced the documents, and they took me to St. Mike's, where I was once again formed and kept for a short stay on the 17th floor.

While on probation, I was set up with a counselor at the Elizabeth Fry Society, Jacquie Jenkins. She heard my story through tears and tried to arrange for my wife and me to get some mediation to resolve the issues. Unfortunately, my wife was under no obligation to participate, and she chose not to do any of the work, so the remediation was for nothing, just a waste of time.

My weekly routine included one or two visits to my probation officer, a visit to Jacquie at the Elizabeth Fry Society once a week, meetings at Sherbourne Health with Carol Baker and the support group once a week, meeting with Dr. Luca Ballerini at Toronto Western Hospital, to talk about my childhood, going to doctor's appointments because now I was also diabetic, visiting the VanDuzer art studio for more art therapy, and abiding by the rules of the shelter and doing assigned chores. I also had to travel three hours each way to Newmarket to try to defend myself in family court with a judge who hated me. All this triggered my anxiety, so I would test my mind by playing Sudoku. There were times when it was easy, but when my mind was messed up, it was nearly impossible for me to finish. Unfortunately, I often got overwhelmed and found myself back in the hospital at St. Mike's or CAMH (the Centre for Addiction and Mental Health) and once at Mount Sinai Hospital.

My life seemed like such a waste of oxygen because I was trying to cope without any resources. Every time I turned around, something would get more complicated and things that I had never thought of before took all of my effort to resolve, mostly because of the medication I was on. I really had to focus to get through each day.

A Midsummer's Dream

by Stefonknee Wolscht, July 7, 2010

It has now been more than a year since I was asked to leave home on May 20, 2009. The year my world imploded as I found myself floating out in the open sea, having been thrown out of my world like a castaway thrown overboard into the abyss. All seemed lost: my family, my home, all my friends, everything is but cherished memories.

Forty-five weeks from September 2, 2009, the day I was called and told that there was a warrant out for my arrest on seven criminal charges. That dreadful call that came three months after my having been told by my wife of twenty-three years to leave my home and my children, while I was sitting in a Toronto library looking for a distraction from my desperate homeless situation. The day my freedom, my dignity, my children, and my entire world were snatched away by a cold justice system that turned slowly, uninterested in facts and feelings, interested only in protocol and procedure.

I have tried countless times and ways to resolve these issues. I've tried unsuccessfully every legal option to get advice and representation. I've tried numerous times in the courtroom to get my side of the story out, only to have the very system that arrested me use every opportunity to shut me down. Alone in a sea of legal jargon, I flounder as I attempt to present my case against all odds. I sat in the legal aid office in the Newmarket Courthouse and begged them to help me. They didn't even give me the time of day. They told me that these charges were too trivial and told me to leave. The Crown is asking for jail time, so I'm not sure what they would consider worth their while to defend. I also contacted the Legal Aid office in Old City Hall in Toronto, and they would not budge either. I left very disappointed and depressed.

On Monday, I will once again find myself alone on the stand, trying to stay calm as I try to defend myself, not from accusations of criminal wrongdoing, but rather from insults and accusations arising from a system hoping to find me guilty of being an embarrassment to the world around me. On Monday, I will answer the judge's questions and be cross-examined by the Crown because I am not entitled to my own lawyer, as would seem fair in any criminal proceedings. On Monday, I trust that God will stand with me and keep me safe, or at least hold me when I lose all hope and give up. On Monday, after the gavel raps and the trial ends, I will either be forever a criminal or, hopefully at least for a short time, innocent until the next allegations tarnish my reputation.

How can I call this nightmare a dream?

It is a dream because it is the only hope I have to ever salvage a relationship with my children again. It is my love story for my children. It is my final attempt to bridge the huge divide created by lies and accusations that has destroyed our family. It is a dream that engulfs a year of our lives, the lives of a loving family, a year of lost memories…

Playing with my seven kids in the river behind our house in Elm Grove

Please listen to "Melodies of Life" by Nobuo Uematsu

(((((((((((((Hugs))))))))))))))))) Steffy

Chapter 4

Ballerini, Baker & Schwartz... & Esprit '09

In August 2009, my GP, Dr. Ramji, referred me to Dr. Luca Ballerini, a counsellor at Toronto Western Hospital. She also referred me to the Gender Identity Clinic at CAMH and to Celia Schwartz and Carol Baker, two counsellors who would work very closely with me. With their support and guidance, I was able to start digging into my past and begin talking about my childhood. Thinking and talking about childhood trauma is very hard and exhausting, and I cried a lot. I did have a lot of good memories of my childhood, but we were there to delve into the issues that were buried deep in my body and mind, the issues that I felt embarrassed to talk about. Dr. Ballerini made it easy to share and took his time by letting me go at my own pace and express my feelings through tears and feelings of anxiety. I cried a lot in his office and used a lot of tissues as he listened.

Mom and Dad, Mary Lou and Paul Sr.

I decided to start at the beginning to give him a little context for the world that I was born into. I was born on June 24, 1963, at Scarborough General Hospital to Paul and Mary Lou Wolscht. I was a new baby brother for my older sister, Monica. I have only one memory before the age of four, but it isn't a good one. I remember waking up to the sound of my father yelling at my mom. I went down the hallway to find him hitting her near the telephone on the wall in the kitchen. I ran to my mom and grabbed onto her leg. My father knocked me down, and as I lay there curled up in a ball at my mom's feet, trying to stay between her and my father, he kicked me in my back. That was the only memory I had of our house on Bayard Avenue in Scarborough. I couldn't have been much more than three because we moved to the farm in Mount Albert when I was four.

My father was working long hours to try to keep the family bakery out of bankruptcy and he was under a lot of stress. His business partners had run the bakery into the ground while he was away getting married in Germany. Now they were gone, and it was up to him alone to keep Montmartre Bakery in business.

Our family bakery, "Montmartre Bakery" Scarborough (Rebuilt 1967)

My father wasn't an angry drunk. In fact, he taught me that it was okay to take a sip of beer and put the cap back on the bottle. He was stressed, and he was the kind of person who wanted to blame someone when anything went wrong. I soon realized that if anything went wrong at his bakery, he would come home and take it out on my mom. In those days, this was considered normal, and women would often be told to just be a good wife, keep a clean house, have the children stay out of their father's way, and put a nice hot meal on the table to keep the peace. Whether it was stress or alcohol, the blame always seemed to be placed on the woman.

When I was four, we moved up to our farm in Mount Albert, which had a driveway that was about a kilometre long. I remember us pulling into the driveway and our car getting stuck almost right away. Our tires were no match for the deep snow and the soft mud of the driveway. We had to get out and walk, and the snow was almost up to my hips. My father led the way. My mom pulled my younger brother, Michael, on a sled, while my sister, Monica, who was older, seemed to be able to walk. I was having trouble walking, and when I couldn't go any farther, my dad became furious and came back towards me. I know that he always considered me to be lazy, but I no longer remember exactly what happened next.

I have since replaced "whatever happened" with a new memory of my older self coming back to pick me up and carry me on my shoulders. This is EMDR. I was taught about EMDR (Eye Movement Desensitization and Reprocessing), a method of replacing an old memory with a new one by tapping on my knees as I visualize a new ending. It's a way to help a person cope with trauma. I highly recommend looking into it if you're dealing with past traumas and need a way to erase them.

I think those were the two incidents that Luca Ballerini was most concerned about for me. Ironically, he wasn't surprised to hear that I had walked in on him when I was fourteen and bigger than my father, yelling at my mother. I ended up coming to my mom's defence and he switched to yelling at me, but I considered myself the black sheep of the family and didn't care if he liked me or hated me. I think that's the last time I ever heard him scream at her, but he would hate me because of that for the rest of my life. That, and my being transgender, was enough to justify to him why I was such an oddball.

There are other times that I experienced trauma in my childhood. One time, when I was helping my father build a fence and was running a fever, my father suddenly became furious at me because he was irritated by the way I was breathing. I remember the sun shining on us and it was a very hot summer day. I was feeling really sick while helping him work and all he could do was complain about the way I was breathing. I often wondered why he hated me so much, and I wondered if I might have been adopted.

Another time, when he came home late from the bakery in Toronto and found a dead steer in the barn, he got us out of bed to scream at us. That kind of thing got to be a regular happening for me as a young child. I remember many times him throwing stuff at me, anything he could get his hands on, whenever something went wrong. On numerous occasions, he threw chunks of firewood or the axe, and once, he threw a pitchfork at me. I remember wishing that he would kill me as I was running away from him. I was scared and afraid of him but part of me wanted to die.

Maria Louisa Heming (1957) would later Mary Lou Wolscht on September 5, 1960

My mother seemed to get the worst of it, and she was afraid of my dad for a long time. I remember once our old John Deere tractor wouldn't start, and we needed it to feed the cows. Our farm had a long feed crib where about eighty cows could spread out to eat corn. When the tractor wouldn't start, my mom set up some planks through the mud between the corn pit and the feed trough so that we could try to feed the cows with a wheelbarrow, which was all in vain. The cows could eat the corn faster than we could deliver it, so there were lots of cattle dangerously jostling around to get access to the corn and making a lot of noise, which added to the chaos. It was frightening to see, but it was sadder to see my mother crying for fear of what would happen when my dad got home. She told us to keep trying to feed them and not give up. All this because the stupid tractor wouldn't start.

Another big part of my childhood was my gender identity. I didn't know the words for it, and I didn't understand what I was or who I was, but I just knew that I identified more with the girls in my class than with the boys. I didn't have the vocabulary to articulate what I was feeling. I remember picture day in grade one when I saw all the girls come to school with pretty new dresses and I was wearing a plain turtleneck and corduroy pants. My parents kept us dressed nicely, but I always envied the girls in my class. I didn't want to dress like a boy; I wanted to become a girl. Clothes for girls seemed so beautiful, and I so badly wished I had been born a girl.

Paul Wolscht Jr. Mount Albert P.S. (September 1969)

My best friend was Kenton Stokes, who lived beside our driveway entrance in a bungalow with his mom, his dad, and his younger brother, Michael. He had a basement full of toys. Among those toys was also a box of hand-me-down clothes from his cousin Laurie. I remember specifically a plaid skirt that fit me. For some reason, I was allowed to change into girls' clothes at their house and play regular boys' games while wearing her old clothes. I remember fishing, playing catch, or horsing around building forts in the forest on our farm. Kenton and I went to Cubs and Scouts, and we would often team up together to sell apples or pizzas to raise money for our troop. Secretly, I wished I could have been a Brownie or a Girl Guide. Kent was a good friend, and we remained best friends until we went on to different high schools. At that point, our friendship dissolved, and we moved on to other things. As for me, I was still questioning why I was a boy, and those questions only became more complicated with the onset of puberty.

Mt. Albert farm Mom with Eric, Paul and Michael (December 1968)

In 1977, I started high school, and I didn't want to take Physical Education because I would be in the changing room with boys. I longed to be in a girls' Phys Ed class, but in those days, it was not possible. So, instead of taking Phys Ed, I took music to get my art credit. I remember early mornings hitchhiking from Mount Albert to Huron Heights Secondary School in Newmarket to get to band practice. I was a mediocre third trombone player who really didn't practice enough to get any good at it, but I was just good enough to be in the stage band. That was pretty cool because there were some very talented people in our stage band: Sam Reid on drums, who would later go on to be the keyboardist and founding member of the band Glass Tiger. Tyler Stewart, who played trumpet, would go on to be the drummer for a little band called The Barenaked Ladies. Needless to say, my playing third trombone in the stage band with the likes of these characters left me wondering why I even bothered. I had no musical talent. I stuck it out for the art credits and went to the early morning practices or stayed after school to get extra help, all in an attempt to have fun being around people who were, in my eyes, really cool.

My friends and I were kind of in the middle of the pack at school; we weren't the cool kids, and we weren't the geeks. We just sort of blended in and did our own thing. I enjoyed science and math, hated English, and loved being in history class. Somehow, in history class, I was able to join in with the cool kids and pull pranks on Mr.

Wilson. When his back was turned while he was writing on the board, we would all start to sing the Pointer Sisters' "Fire." Without turning around or missing a beat, Mr. Wilson would always say, "Quiet, you idiots!!" We would all burst out laughing. Mr. Wilson made learning fun, so much fun that I took history in all four of my high school years.

I made it through high school, mostly focusing on auto mechanics. I had hoped to go into something like engineering, but my father insisted I learn a trade. So, I chose auto mechanics and after graduating high school in 1981, I finished my apprenticeship by 1985 and became a licensed auto mechanic.

Life on my father's farm wasn't all bad. In fact, I have a lot of great memories: I remember sitting in fields watching cows graze in the hot summer sun, finding shade under an apple tree, picking up apples, and taking a few bites only to throw the rest of the apples to the cows for them to eat; lying on cedar rail beds that we made in our forts and feeling the breeze come through the cedar trees and cool us on those hot summer days. We had a creek running through our property and I remember countless hours skating on the ice or walking up the creek because there was less snow on the ice than on the fields. Winters back in the seventies had a lot more snow than we get today. I also enjoyed the farm with our dog, Tanya, going for long walks to check on the cows and imagining different worlds and different adventures. We also had a red and white boat that my dad would tow behind our car to take us up to Lake Simcoe to go boating or waterskiing at Sibbald Point.

Heading up to Sibbald Point Provincial Park, Lake Simcoe

On the farm, I learned to drive at a very young age, and it didn't take very long before I had one of our old cars as a field burner. At ten years old, I could drive our gold Chrysler New Yorker around fields or up and down our long driveway, pretending I was driving on a city road, windows down and the radio blasting, having a wonderful time.

At one point, my parents decided to get a swimming pool, which wasn't very common in those days. It was so nice to have a pool where friends could come up and swim with us. On more than one occasion, we would find a cow or a pig swimming in the pool and that would turn into quite the ordeal to get them out safely. Summers were always more fun once we had the pool. We brought in a lot of hay and quite often, after a few loads were unloaded into the sweltering heat of the barn, we would run to the house for a quick dip in the pool. It was so refreshing, and it was a nice break. Having a pool really made a difference, and things were looking a lot better by then.

Being on a farm also meant learning to use a gun to shoot groundhogs so as to stop them from digging holes in the pastures, which could injure the cows and horses. By the time I was twelve, I had to learn how to slaughter cows. Almost every Saturday, we would shoot a cow that a customer had chosen. I was expected to pitch in with the slaughtering by helping skin, gut, and quarter the cow. Touching a dead animal when you're a child can be pretty traumatic, and I remember being hesitant to step forward and pitch in at the beginning. It was really gross, and for a twelve-year-old, it was pretty yucky to see all the bloody guts of a slaughtered cow. With time, I would imagine that I was just touching a candle because the cool flesh of the cow had the texture of wax. I was also very conscious not to touch my face after having touched a dead animal. I kind of thought that it would give me cooties, and I didn't want any of the dead animal's blood anywhere on my body other than my hands. After a while, it was no longer a big deal, and slaughtering cows became a routine part of our Saturday mornings. We would usually finish before lunch and by one o'clock, we'd go down to the Stouffville Stockyards for the afternoon. It was on those visits to Stouffville as a child that I started collecting coins and banknotes, a hobby I've passed on to my children and grandchildren.

Having had to use a gun to kill things as a child discouraged me from ever owning a gun myself later in life. My kids lived in a home that was gun-free, but somehow, they own guns now and go hunting. I often wonder: *where did I go wrong?*

It was also around twelve years old that I got my first paper route with the *Toronto Star* and started delivering newspapers to the houses in Mount Albert every morning before school. It meant a lot of extra cash that I would use to buy a calf or pig to raise and sell for a profit. It was nice to have extra pocket money to buy trinkets, expand my coin collection, and buy my own clothes, and I remember Levi's were a special acquisition. Also, the money helped pay for my trip to Germany later that year. Once, at an auction, I invested my earnings to buy twenty-five toilets for one dollar each. I needed to convince a local trucker to deliver them to Stouffville Stockyards the next Saturday and we split the profits when I sold the whole lot for $100.00, which was a lot of money back then.

I celebrated my thirteenth birthday at 30,000 feet in the air above the Atlantic Ocean, flying to Germany with my sister, Monica, for a summer vacation with my uncles, aunts, and cousins.

At midnight, a stewardess came up to me and asked if I wanted to spend my birthday morning in the cockpit with the pilot, co-pilot, and navigator. I was excited to be able to spend some time in the front of the plane with all those gauges, blinking lights, and switches while chatting with the crew about living life on a farm and them telling me what it's like to fly a plane. We had a great summer with my relatives and their friends in Germany.

At this age, I was still very much into girls' dresses. I'd sneak my sister's clothes from the hand-me-down closet, clothes intended for my cousins, and I'd hide them between my mattress and box spring. I especially treasured a long yellow polyester dress that I thought was so fancy, and it made me feel special. I once went so far as to ask my mom if I could paint a rainbow in my room and she said I could, but I would have to paint it on the inside of my closet door, so my dad would never see it. I ended up painting the door white on the inside and then painted a rainbow, a unicorn, and flowers and later added some smiley face stickers. I could open the door when I wore dresses and enter a whole new world. So, ironically, I guess I really did come out of the closet.

My mom was okay with me wearing Monica's old dresses; she would even wash them and put them back between the mattress and box spring. But she did ask me to never let my dad see them because he would not understand, and she worried for my safety. I kept that promise for a long time, actually until after she had passed away. One day, shortly after Maria and I had separated, I was dressed as a girl and heading to a club when my dad called to see if his mechanic son could get his tractor started. I thought *I'm not heading back to the apartment to get changed*, so I drove over in a skirt and a blouse. That was the first time he ever saw me dressed as a girl. His only comment was, "Oh, this is like on Oprah." Too which I responded, "Yes, something like that." It would be shortly after this that he disowned me, and we never reconciled or talked again.

Growing up a farm kid was both hard work and fun. It gave me time to be alone in the house when I could put on a dress when my dad was away and just be a girl for a while in my room. Oh, how I wished that I could have just stayed a girl, but most of my time was spent doing alpha male farm work with my younger brothers, Michael, Eric, and Robert.

We all did the regular farm stuff, and every summer, we'd bale about 300 acres of hay all over Mount Albert. We would finish the first cut just in time to start the second cut. My dad would go fifty-fifty with the property owners. We would cut and bale the hay on their fields and give the owners half the hay. It was difficult, hard work in the hot summer sun, and quite often in fields that were marshy, full of mosquitoes, and yielding poor quality hay. Lots of weeds and snakes would go through the baler. In the fall, we would harvest corn to fill our small silo and our corn pit with enough corn to keep the cows fed through the winter. The smells upstairs of the barn of fresh hay and the smell of corn in the silo that had just been harvested were very therapeutic and still bring back memories, but the smell of manure in the bottom of the barn was disgustingly horrible. Sometimes, we would need to go into the barn with our winter boots and I remember the smell of melting, manure-covered snow stinking up the school bus—that was embarrassing.

One of the best things on the farm was the delivery of Rowntree's chocolates for the cows. Danny Barkey would randomly show up throughout the winter and into the spring and sell us truckloads of chocolates for $80 each. In every truckload, we would get big bags of Smarties, Coffee Crisps, Aero Bars, and Black Magic chocolates for the cows. Needless to say, a lot of this chocolate got eaten by us five kids and also by town kids coming up to help themselves to the chocolates from our barn. There was even a time we started a business of bringing little baggies of Smarties to sell them at our high school. That was quickly stopped by the principal once our Smarties were being used as ammunition in food fights all over the school. Smarties make excellent bullets.

Wolscht kids being silly in our old yellow John Deere tractor with
visitors from Germany (1972)

My dad was very good at making money. A friend of ours once said to me, "Your dad could fall into a pile of shit and find a dollar." At some point, my dad sold his bakery to one of his employees, a family friend we called Uncle Joe, so he could buy our second and third farms. The one we called 11A, where we grew corn, had a campground at the back that our local Cubs and Scouts could use as a camping site. On the other farm, in Sandford, we grew oats and barley so that we didn't have to buy our grains anymore. My father even bought the local grain mill when it went out of business, and we spent the next two years emptying the silos at

Mount Albert's Feed & Farm Supply to supplement our cows' nutrition. As kids, we got to explore all the cracks and crevices that were opened as we augured the grain out of the building. My dad also made extra money helping gentleman farmers with their crops. I remember us helping neighbours harvest their corn and hay. When I was fourteen, one neighbour even hired me to pump gas for him at his convenience store, Country Fair in Mount Albert, my first easy physical job.

I lived with my parents on the home farm until 1985. I was working at that time as an apprentice and helping my parents build a new house. We were shingling the roof when I realized that there was no bedroom for me. It was clear my dad wanted me to move out. As soon as I finished helping him build the house, he rented the old farmhouse out and I had to move. Luckily, I found a place to live with my friend Rick Callaghan, who was moving down to Scarborough into his recently deceased grandfather's house. Rick was my best man at our wedding.

***

Luca Ballerini was a good listener. Week after week, he listened to my stories as I cried in his office and got these things off my chest. He suggested that I go back to St. Mike's hospital and have them reassess the diagnosis of bipolar from Dr. Robinson and

Dr. Ooi. My diagnosis was eventually changed to Situational Depression and Complex PTSD, so I was taken off Seroquel (Quetiapine), a mind-numbing bipolar medication that left me always confused and scared.

At CAMH, I often tried to explain what life is like from my vantage point, isolated from my children and siblings because I'm transgender, but it fell on deaf ears. Transitioning is really hard for everyone, and CAMH did not seem very sympathetic to our plight.

Celia Schwartz was another very kind counsellor with St. Michael's Hospital. She helped clients navigate the medical and legal system to find their way through gender dysphoria. Celia also helped me with my depression and went out of her way to make sure that I was treated with respect by any agencies that were there to help me. She would see me weekly and talk about my gender identity issues, which I would share with her to learn more about who I was and what I was feeling. She's the counsellor who wrote my gender dysphoria letter that got me access to the gender identity clinic at CAMH.

Unfortunately, at that time, the clinic was run by Dr. Kenneth Zucker, who believed in reparative and electric shock therapy, which was often used to torture LGBT people in an attempt to make us conform to what society expected us to be. He also had a 240-question questionnaire that he made trans people fill out, asking if they were pedophiles, engaged in bestiality, or were a threat to society. It was very humiliating and triggering to be going through all these questions on forms that endorsed old stereotypes. Dr. Zucker's receptionist, Suzette, was also extremely mean, and she would often correspond with me using "Mr. Paul Wolscht" in the salutation, which meant the letters would be sent back with an explanation that they were mailing it to a women's shelter, not a men's shelter. Celia took it upon herself to correct these mistakes and make me feel more like a human being again.

***

Before I moved out of my home, I had registered to go to a transgender retreat on the last weekend of April 2009. I went to Gananoque for a transgender weekend put on by Gender Mosaic of Ottawa, organized by Amanda Ryan and Sophia D'Aoust. Once there, I got to meet other transgender people and we had a beautiful time doing stuff at the hotel, living as women. We also had outings like a Thousand Islands cruise, where we were all dressed up in our best evening gowns as we navigated the St. Lawrence River. The weather was hot and humid, but the boat was moving fast enough to create a breeze and we were all comfortable dressed in our finery. I wore a black dress that I had brought with me as well as jewellery that I had borrowed from Maria.

I cannot describe how liberating it is to be free to express something that has been kept bottled up for so long. It's like keeping the lid on a pressure cooker and at any time, the whole thing could explode but going to this retreat helped release some of the pressure. This was an amazing way to rid myself of guilt and shame and allow my inner girl to finally be free.

After the cruise, we all went back to the hotel and socialized over dinner. I remember that we ate pasta that I wasn't able to finish, or maybe I chose not to finish because I became aware of my dress size and worried about my figure in my bathing suit in the pool that night. It was a lot to take in getting to be a girl all day, every day, and needless to say, I was very excited and happy to finally be able to express my inner feminine self for more than a few hours.

The following day, we had a team of makeup artists come in from the local Shoppers Drug Mart to teach us about makeup, care of wigs and to help us get ready for a fashion show that evening. On the way to Gananoque, I stopped off at Sears to be fitted for two dresses that I would be wearing at the fashion show. I loved those two outfits; in fact, after the fashion show, I bought the dresses and I still have them today. One was a yellow floral dress, and the other was a yellow sweater with a yellow floral skirt. Both of them were very spring like, excellent for the heat of that time of year.

I tell a lot of people that my favourite colour is pink, but for some reason, I get a lot of compliments when I wear yellow. This reminded me of my first dress that I wore, which was my older sister's hand-me-down—I still remember that dress and wonder whatever happened to it.

Before the weekend ended, we went to the local casino where we experienced some harassment from the casino security for using the women's washroom. That was a bit of a reality check, that not everyone was accepting of trans women. The next day, we said our goodbyes and headed back home. A week later, on May 11, I was heading to Victoria, British Columbia, to go to Esprit '09, a conference in Port Angeles, in Washington state.

Maria encouraged me to go away for a weekend and now for an entire week. We called them "Stephanie vacations," and it was not uncommon for me to go on mini-Stephanie vacations but never this far or this long. I had never travelled by air as a woman before. I went with a friend, Stephanie Williams, and we had no idea what it would be like to travel across the country by air, going through security at two airports, and taking a ferry into the United States in women's dresses. As it turned out, we worried about something that was not a big deal; all was fine, and we got to Port Angeles without a hitch. At the ferry terminal, we found ourselves waiting with four strapping young men who were black and blue from fighting with locals the night before, which worried us, but there was nothing to worry about there, either. They were very intrigued by what we were doing. At the United States customs desk, we were asked by two young men if we had anything to declare. I just passed them my suitcase and told them nothing more than panties, skirts, and dresses. They waved us through, obviously quite embarrassed.

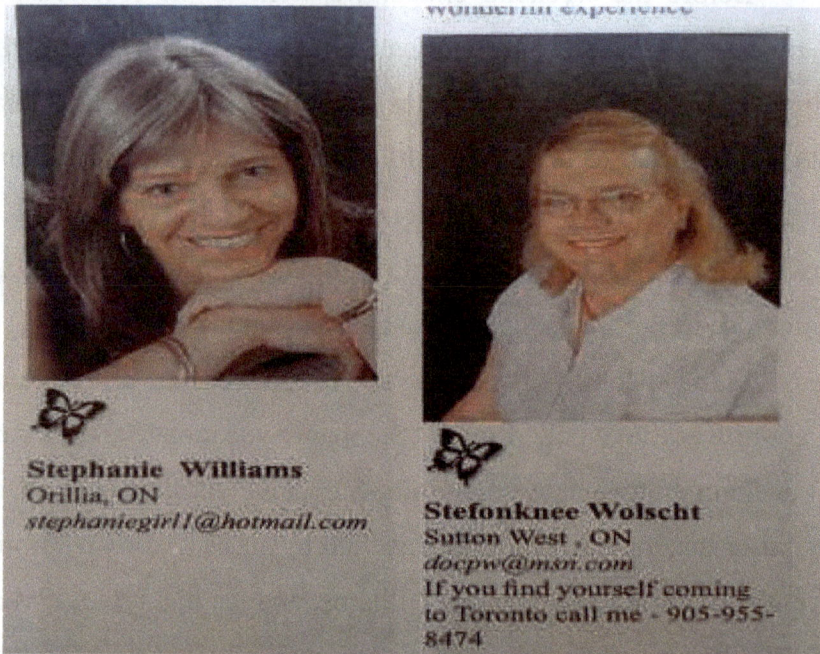

Stephanie Williams
Orillia, ON
stephaniegirl1@hotmail.com

Stefonknee Wolscht
Sutton West , ON
docpw@msn.com
If you find yourself coming to Toronto call me - 905-955-8474

Stephanie and Stefonknee at Esprit '09 Port Angeles Washington
(April 2009)

I ventured into a biker bar on the first day in Port Angeles and played pool with a couple of women, me dressed in a cute top and leather mini skirt. Two men at the bar started buying me drinks, which concerned me, so I went up to explain to them that I was married and that I was not into men, to which they responded they weren't looking to go home with me but instead wanted to know how I got those two women to let me play pool with them. I laughed and responded, "If you wear a black mini-skirt, then I'm sure they'll let you play pool as well."

The week was amazing, but most of the convention attendees stayed in the hotel for the entire seven days. I, on the other hand, made a point of getting out to meet the local townsfolk and introduced myself to various business owners such as Stefonknee. It was here at Esprit '09 that I got the name "Stefonknee" because, as it turned out, there were five Stephanies at the conference, so we messed up the spelling of everyone's name and I became known as Stefonknee with an F'n K.

The more I explored Port Angeles, the more I came to love the quaint little town with its beautiful inhabitants who made me feel welcome everywhere I went.

At a local bar called Liars, I was a hit from the minute I walked in. I was asked by one woman if my breasts were real, at which I immediately reached inside my dress and pulled one out to show her the silicone falsies that I was wearing. She was so impressed she asked if she could try them on and her husband loved the new fuller figure it gave her. The next thing I knew, my silicone boobs were making their way around the bar as most of the women wanted to see what they looked like with size DD silicone falsies. It was karaoke night and I got up to sing "American Pie," while playing an inflatable electric guitar. It wasn't long before a bunch of women came up and joined me on stage as we muddled our way through, off-key and in tears, laughing hysterically to the beat of the band.

The next day at the conference, we were told about the etiquette of being in Port Angeles and that we should remain in the hotel for our safety. I questioned this advice because I had had such a good experience the previous night, and I wanted to go back out and meet more people and mingle with the local residents. A few of the girls were surprised to hear that I had gone into the village, but when I told them that I was heading back out to do some shopping that afternoon, four of them joined me as we left the conference and went back downtown to shop.

Shopping was great fun, and we went to a restaurant as girls for lunch. We met lots of beautiful people—in fact, we were the talk of the town. People had heard about me going to Liars the night before and they wanted to meet this strange new person in Port Angeles. I found myself handing out business cards with my picture on them to locals throughout the village and told them that my business card would get them into our talent show, which was held that evening at a local community hall.

Most Inspirational Award goes to Stefonknee Wolscht (April 2009)

Little did I know that about fifty local residents came to the talent show and set themselves up on the balcony until the first song was played by a transgender rock band. Immediately, they came storming down the stairs and started grabbing trans women from their seats and coaxing them onto the dance floor. The night was a huge success, even though I left early to start a bit of a scene for the local country folk in the neighbouring town. As it turned out, we were a big hit wherever we went.

The week's festivities ended with a gala on a Saturday night. Just prior to the gala, I found out that my daughter Chavonne had given birth to a healthy, beautiful baby girl, Rebecca, a little sister for my three-year-old darling grandson, Jacob. At the gala, awards were handed out for some local sponsors as well as a monarch butterfly brooch that was awarded to the most inspirational attendee, which I ended up winning and taking home with me for the year. My friend Stephanie Williams was voted runner-up: not too bad for a couple of Canadian trans women in the USA. Between the birth of my granddaughter and winning the award, I found myself crying tears of joy most of that evening.

On the last day, I was invited to go to church with one of the elderly local women whom I'd met at the gala. She picked me up on Sunday morning and took me to her Catholic church, which was a huge hit as well. My being a Grand Knight in our K of C Council 8026 in Sutton interested the local Knights of Columbus members in Port Angeles; I think they thought I went to Knights of Columbus meetings dressed as a girl.

The flight home was uneventful, but unfortunately, when we landed in Toronto, we were greeted by a very angry Maria, who had agreed to pick us up at the airport and take us back home. I was very excited to meet Rebecca, my new granddaughter, but Maria was uncharacteristically quiet and refused to talk to me. Once we got to my place, I said my goodbyes to Stephanie, and then I went with Maria to visit Chavonne and meet my new granddaughter.

Stefonknee with her new granddaughter, Rebecca (April 18, 2009)

I noticed that my kids were all very abrupt with me and seemed cross. I had come home very excited to meet my beautiful new granddaughter, but it was not what I was hoping it would be. Something was wrong, and it seemed like I was a stranger in Chavonne's house. We went home early because Chavonne wanted to put the kids to bed. When I got home, I was exhausted and went off to bed. I didn't realize it at the time, but Maria never came to bed; she slept on the couch that night. The next day, I ate my breakfast, and I started repairing cars again in the shop. When the day was over, I ate my dinner alone and went back to bed, still tired from the week in Port Angeles.

At two a.m. on May 20, I realized I was alone in bed, so I went downstairs and told Maria that she could have the bed and I would sleep on the couch, to which she responded that I needed "to stop being transgender or leave." My heart sank and I felt defeated. I ended up getting into my car and drove away, looking for a bridge to crash into, but being unable to find a way to smash up the car, I sat on a dead-end road crying. I finally got home around five a.m. to see my best friend, Peter Bunnik, who was there consoling my wife. I just went upstairs, packed a bag, and left for the city to couch surf at friends' houses in Toronto. Thinking back on it all, I realized that the entire month was a lie. It wasn't safe to express my gender identity, it was all too much, and now I was paying the price for being so open about who I really was.

On June 6, I found a room in an apartment in Toronto as Stefonknee. Unemployed, I tried unsuccessfully to create my new life; I was unable to re-establish myself due to the many hurdles placed in my path. By July 23, I had given up all hope and found myself hospitalized for attempted suicide caused by depression and isolation.

On August 6, when I moved into the Gerstein Crisis Centre, I began to get counselling for depression at Sherbourne Health.

On August 15, I moved into a homeless shelter in Toronto. While there, I attempted to collect my belongings from the room I'd rented but found that the locks had been changed on the apartment, so I asked Toronto police to help me get my belongings. Brenda, the woman on the lease, ignored the police when they knocked on her door. She said in a text that my wife had come and picked everything up and there was nothing there to collect, but she would not let us into the apartment. As it turned out, she had sold all my stuff while I was locked up at St. Mike's Hospital.

By August 28, my wife cut off all communication while a retired cop from our church set about finding ways to have me arrested to block me from getting access to my home and family.

That was when I received a call from York Regional Police stating that they had a warrant for my arrest. I turned myself in and was arrested on seven criminal charges stemming from actions taken by Mr. Tracey and my wife that interpreted regular family interactions over the previous five years as criminal offences. Despite forty-six years of being a law-abiding citizen and having a twenty-three-year marriage without incident that included daily police visits for coffee breaks or car repairs, I now found myself behind bars.

I believe the criminal charges were an attempt to alienate me from my children, something known as PAS (Parental Alienation Syndrome). Keep in mind that three months had passed since I had left peacefully, hoping to return once we could better understand my gender issues. I had moved to Toronto and was busy volunteering and speaking at Ryerson, U of T, and various trans-positive spaces throughout the city. I had enrolled to begin some upgrading courses at George Brown College and was trying to move on with my life. I

107

believe that my wife, with the encouragement of Fr. Herman Dias and Rick Tracey, used the legal system to prevent my children from continuing to have a relationship with their father, even though I was their primary caregiver during our marriage. Fr. Dias has since sent me emails stating that I am possessed by the evil one for being transgender and depressed. Later, Mr. Tracey made it very clear to me at various times while waiting in Newmarket Court that my presenting as female was, in his opinion, the primary reason for their actions and for my arrest, which I seemed to be overlooking and ignoring. The other charges were for things that happened over the years that seemed innocent until twisted around to sound much worse than they were and construed to have been done in anger.

I was denied legal aid from the office in Newmarket and again at Old City Hall in Toronto. I was continuously tormented and had to endure discriminatory comments from my family, strangers, the police, the crown attorney, and even from the judges as I stood alone before a legal system intent on punishing me for being different and an embarrassment. I was completely overwhelmed and alone, suffering from depression and being marginalized. It seemed that I was defending my very right to exist. Up until this point, I had taken for granted the respect and privileges that I had once enjoyed as a white male, when I kept my gender a secret from everyone outside of our home. Despite my never before having had a criminal record or hurting my wife or children, I was portrayed as a dangerous criminal who caused my wife and children to fear for their lives, even after months of abiding by all the bail conditions and getting counselling and medical attention for my extreme depression.

By early December, I qualified for transitional housing and began taking testosterone blockers to begin my transition. By January 2010, I began estrogen hormone therapy after realizing that I had lost my children and all that I had worked forty-six years to accomplish. What else did I have to lose?

Stefonknee in her room at Joubert House (March 20, 2010)

At this point, speaking about transgender rights was still very new in Canada. There was protection within the city of Toronto, but we had not achieved human rights protection in Ontario or throughout the rest of the country. Very few Canadians had the vocabulary to describe us or knew why we needed people to use the right pronouns when addressing transgender people. This work that we were doing was very new and very exciting, but it was too little too late for my situation.

I felt very connected to the city that I now called home and knew that we had a lot of allies who would rally with us and demand the government take action. This work needed to be done and I had nothing left to lose, so I thought, *why not join in the fight to try to get us human rights?*

Carol Baker, my counsellor at Sherbourne Health, scheduled me in for an hour each week for counselling as well as two hours of group therapy in a women's art group called "Outside the Lines." Carol was a very passionate counsellor who treated all her clients like they were family. Unfortunately, a few months later, I lost access to Carol when she retired and moved to Montreal to be with her daughter and her first grandchild.

These were some of my darkest days when I felt the whole world was against me. It was the actions of a few good people that brought me to a place where I could make new friends and be treated like a human being.

The only thing that I can add to what happened to me at CAMH is that I would later meet a nice doctor at the 519 Centre in Toronto, Dr. Nicola Brown, who looked into my file and immediately called me to apologize on behalf of the health centre. She later sent me a written apology for what they had put me through.

Here is what I once shared with the medical staff at CAMH...

Three Lines? / You / Me /?

I see three perpendicular lines in my mind. Between two lines that run parallel to each other, I see everything that you see and believe to be real, but I exist between the second and third lines: you cannot see me. You know I am there because you can hear me but do not understand me. Because you cannot comprehend what I am saying, you fear me. I am very different from you. I look different, I think different, I sound different, I live differently than you... but I am NOT different! I feel pain, my skin bleeds, my eyes turn red when I cry...

Why does everyone make me cry?

Please leave me alone behind your lines and let me be! I am isolated from all of you, so why do you fear me? It makes me sad to think that I scare you. I don't want to be like the people on your side of the line. I only want to help. I wish people would just take what I say, think, and write and just accept it as my reality—and it really is my reality—but it seems to be very odd to you. I don't want to change or influence your world. I just want to document what I see from the outside.

I wonder, will it ever change? I hope someday someone will listen. I know others came before me, others who were like me, and they were unsuccessful. I know I have been unsuccessful, too. Perhaps someday, someone will be able to convince you that the world is much bigger than what you see between your two lines. I don't know and can't prove what came before us. I don't know and can't predict what will come after we leave. All I know is time exists, but we can't see it. Perhaps if we have enough faith to trust each other, then there is hope. If there is no hope, it is because we exist in a world that we made hopeless!

Ironically, we all want the same things…

To be loved, to coexist. To try and enjoy every moment. To be pain-free. To leave something behind after we are gone. To be respected. To be understood. Etc.

In reality, we get … Hurt. Rejected. Oppressed. Judged. Misunderstood, Forgotten. Etc.

Why don't we just believe in each other and accept that each of us is unique with special gifts that we want to share to help others enjoy life and feel loved? When I'm gone, my life will have meant nothing. When I'm gone, someone will cry. When I'm gone, I will find peace.

Stefonknee Wolscht,

October 13, 2012, CAMH

Chapter 5
Fifteen Years 1986 – 2001

I think it's important that you get an idea of what life was like for me with my wife and my children in the early years of our marriage. After I became licensed as a mechanic, I worked at various shops throughout Toronto as a Volkswagen/Audi mechanic specializing in electrical problems. During my apprenticeship, I had an opportunity to buy a piece of land up in Georgina Township, on a quiet road in the small hamlet of Elm Grove. The property at 470 Catering Road had a river at the back that was deep enough for boating, rafting, and swimming. I would often go up there to camp out on weekends and cut the grass. Over time, I put in a gravel driveway, electricity, a well, and a septic system.

While I was working as a mechanic, Maria was attending York University, getting her teaching certificate to teach elementary level French. I remember going to visit her at the Glendon College campus in my work clothes many evenings and being able to put on some of Maria's clothes, to relax and be a little more feminine. After we married, we moved into her parent's house, which was large enough to accommodate two families. I stopped working in the city and started fixing cars in my father-in-law's barn. Soon after the birth of our first baby, Chavonne, we bought a mobile home, moved it onto my beautiful Georgina lot, and hooked it up to the well, power, and septic system. It was in that new home that we welcomed Amanda into our lives.

We began construction of our house in front of the trailer a year later. Life was pretty complicated for me at that point. I was still running my shop in my father-in-law's barn. If I wasn't busy fixing cars, we were busy building the house with the help of relatives, and in the middle of the night, I was still delivering *Toronto Star* newspapers. All the while raising the kids in the shop and in the mobile home.

Construction of Wolscht house (1992) 470 Catering Rd. Sutton (Elm Grove)

Amanda and Christopher playing in backyard

Life was so innocent and pure in those early days. I felt like I was on top of the world. With Maria's encouragement, I was able to have Stephanie time in Toronto at a place called Take a Walk On the Wildside. Maria and I would go down to Wildside and I would change into a dress and put on my wig and makeup while she mingled with other wives and girlfriends. Wildside was also the home of the Canadian Cross Dressers Club, CCDC. A place where I could meet other transgender people like me. It was amazing because, back before the internet, I was very isolated and hardly had any sense of a trans community. Wildside was like a real chat room where cross-dressers and trans people could meet in person.

When Chavonne was about three years old, we stopped going down to Wildside as a couple. I still had some Stephanie time with my friends while Maria stayed home with the babies. But we were worried they might get confused if they saw me walking around in women's clothes, so I always changed in Toronto at the club.

Wildside was a fantastic treat for me, and on my way to the city, I would often stop in at thrift stores or plus-size women's stores to check what they had that I might like. I never had an issue shopping for women's clothes except once in Quebec when I was asked to leave a store because I was a man. Most stores were grateful to have the business, and my money was as good as anyone's. The other thing I started doing was wearing a skirt while I was delivering the papers in the middle of the night, when I was alone in the van and didn't have to worry about anyone finding out.

At Wildside, I made a lot of great friends. After we changed into our feminine personas, we would all go out for dinner and then come back for karaoke and drinks at the club. Some of the women like Melissa, Tammy, Valerie, Janice, and Shadmith are still my friends today. We grew up in a time when Toronto Police at 52 Division would persecute us just for walking the streets in women's clothes. They would be watching for us to come out of the club in dresses to arrest us, beat us, or rape us at Cherry Beach.

If you listen to the words of "The Cherry Beach Express," by the Pukka Orchestra, you'll see what we lived through at this time in history. They put words to our reality and what the Toronto Police did to trans women, cross-dressers and drag queens.

Another thing that happened in the mid-1990s was a triple killing described by the *Toronto Sun* as the "Degenerate Scum Murders," the account of Marcello Palma's murder of three transgender sex workers in under two hours. He shot each one in the head with a .357 Magnum.

As you can tell, these were very scary times to be transgender in Canada. If things were this bad in a big city like Toronto, you can imagine the pressure to conform in rural towns and smaller cities. Everyone seemed to have misconceptions of what transgender people were and they weren't afraid to lash out at us.

For me, going out as a woman got too dangerous and it would come to an end as I got busy with building the house and raising our children. As the kids got older, I had to put my cross-dressing on the back burner. For the next fifteen years, I focused on being a parent and a provider. Maria finished her teacher's degree by the time Michael was born and worked as a French teacher in the

Catholic school board, before starting to work at Pickering College. It wasn't something I had planned to do. It's just that our family was growing so fast and there was so much work that needed to be done that left little time for me to express my feminine side in Toronto. I have no regrets; the time spent with my children was priceless. I think if I had to do it all over again, I wouldn't change a thing.

When Christopher was born, in 1991, we moved into our new home, where we had a proper nursery for the baby and the girls could have their own rooms. The house wasn't finished, but the furnace, the plumbing, the kitchen, and five bathrooms were all installed, and the carpeting was laid, so we had the semblance of a house. This was about the time that I got meningitis and had to be hospitalized, so construction and finishing touches were slowed down for almost a year.

For our first Christmas in the house, we put up our Christmas tree down in the basement and made that space a giant playroom for the children to ride their tricycles and their pedal cars and play with their dolls. We made it cozy with a wood stove and some carpeting in the play area. We were living a simple life, but it was a lot of fun.

The kids loved playing in the basement in the winter and playing in the backyard in the summer. We built a huge two-story playhouse with a sandbox on the first floor and a kitchenette on the second floor, plus a slide spiralling down to the ground. It had a swing set attached to one side of it. Many of the community children and a lot of neighbours' kids came to play in our backyard. Eventually, we added a volleyball net, basketball nets, a tether ball, and a little spring-bottomed duck that the kids could ride.

Backyard playhouses at 470 Catering Road (1995)

I had moved my shop from my father-in-law's farm to our home garage, which I had built big enough for that purpose so I could add a hoist and all the equipment needed to do car repairs from home. Having my shop in our garage allowed me to take care of the children while I was working and, being right there, I could easily get whatever they needed from the house. Around this time, the baby monitor was invented, so I was able to put the babies to sleep and listen to their breathing while I worked on cars. When they woke up, I would go inside and play with them.

This went on for almost fifteen years. I got to be a mom during the day, even though I looked like a dad, and often spent the evenings finishing car repairs. It was amazing being a parent to little kids. They look at the world with fresh eyes and they teach us to see the wonder in everything around us. I would often take the kids on canoe rides down the river to go raspberry picking. They loved to grab the berries that were growing on the shore, so much so that sometimes it was all I could do to keep the boat from capsizing. We laughed a lot, sang a lot and did a lot of silly stuff.

We had built the house to accommodate a large family and it didn't take very long for Michael, Nicole, Peter, and Robert to join us on our adventures. Our house proved large enough to fit all seven kids nicely and the property's acreage provided play space for every child in Elm Grove. Every Christmas, we invited all our relatives to our house at their convenience. We held an open house the entire week between Christmas and New Year's. This worked out well for our whole family; Maria and I avoided packing up seven children and heading out to everyone's houses and then coming back home with sleepy, crying babies and kids who needed to be carried up to bed. Instead, we would spend hours in front of the fireplace, eating, drinking, and laughing and the kids could play for hours with all their friends and cousins.

Our community of Elm Grove was a very quiet and safe place to raise children. Most of the families on our street had young kids, and as our girls got older, they started to babysit for the neighbours. It was a pleasure to see all the kids growing up together. We had community events at a one-room schoolhouse, which the neighbourhood had restored. Later, it was used as a daycare centre for the local kids. Most of the neighbours liked coming over to our house with my automotive shop right there, where they could get their cars and boats and snowmobiles fixed. The neighbours' kids loved playing in the backyard with our kids and it didn't take long for us to become good friends with everyone on the street.

Also, there were ten cousins on each side of the family and with our seven, that made for quite the gang. We purchased a timeshare at Horseshoe Valley for the week of the March break. At the resort, the kids could learn to ski and snowboard, swim in the indoor/outdoor pool, and have a lot of fun in the snow. We would invite all the cousins to come and visit us during the March Break so they, too, could enjoy the amenities. This ended up being so successful that we bought another timeshare week during the Christmas vacation break from school.

Skiing at Horseshoe Valley, Dad and Peter (March 2002)

At one point, we had kids in four different schools. It was quite the adventure on parent-teacher nights. Maria and I had to divide the schools up between us and really hoof it in order to meet with all the teachers.

Along with school sports and music, we enrolled our kids in figure skating, hockey, and soccer, plus Sparks and Brownies. To say we were busy was an understatement. We were always rushing around to get to the next event for one or another of our seven kids. Being involved at every level of extracurricular activities meant we had a lot of meetings to attend as well.

Our family was also very active in our church. I was a lecturer; Maria was a Eucharistic minister; the kids were altar servers, sang with the church choir, and attended the church youth group. As a family, we were all busy with the Knights of Columbus. The church youth group was invited many times by Gordon and Martha Krupp to visit Montrose, Michigan, to take part in Youth to Youth, a Christian young people's retreat. We really enjoyed those trips to Michigan as a family. We invited this group to come and stay with us when the Pope visited Toronto. And what an adventure that turned out to be: we had fifty-two people in our house for ten days in July 2002, because the group needed to stay together as they were doing catechetical sessions for World Youth Day. At the end of the World Youth Day activities, we were exhausted, but we experienced many miracles and blessings. One of the miracles was that the Pope would be visiting Köln, Germany, a short distance from where my cousin Reinhold Wolscht lived with his family in Bad Honnef. I contacted my cousin and he agreed to take all of us in for the German World Youth Day in 2005. And once again, it turned out to be a miraculous experience with us doing catechetical sessions in Germany as well. Our family became very good friends with everyone who was part of Youth to Youth in Michigan.

My cousin Reinhold Wolscht and family hosting our family and the Youth to Youth from Montrose, Michigan, at his house in Bad Honnef, Germany, for World Youth Day 2005

With my membership in the Knights of Columbus came a lot of volunteering opportunities, and our family pitched in to help as a team. In those days, kids needed eighty hours of volunteer time to graduate high school, and my kids exceeded that twenty-fold. One week, Amanda volunteered eighty hours with the Knights of Columbus at the Sutton Fair from Thursday to Sunday. We were exhausted but we loved getting up and putting on the coffee at five a.m. and staying there serving food till one a.m. every day. I think these times defined us as a family. And everyone in the community knew about our volunteering throughout Georgina.

As the kids got older, they showed an aptitude towards music. We could have had a family choir, they harmonized so perfectly together. We could almost have had an orchestra, too. Chavonne learned to play the saxophone, Amanda played flute, piano, guitar, and French horn, Christopher played guitar, Michael played drums and saxophone, and Nicole learned to play the violin. I'm not sure if Peter and Robert ever picked up an instrument because by the time they were old enough to learn an instrument, Maria and I had separated and I lost all contact.

As you can see, the first fifteen years of marriage were really busy, and I didn't have very much time to focus on my cross-dressing or being Stephanie. It was more than enough to fix cars from home during the day and play the role of Mom to the seven amazing kids in the morning before school and in the afternoons before dinner.

Time Travel

by Stefonknee Wolscht

I often dream about travelling through time, revisiting the past and to look into the future. I believe in reincarnation. I believe we've all lived a thousand lives, and we will continue to be reincarnated to experience what the future has in store for us.

As we travel through time, one day at a time, we live to experience and to learn from our experiences. Time, I believe, is on a continuum, like holding a ruler in front of you; on the left is the beginning of time and on the right is the end of time, and all of time exists in between these two points. We enter and exit at different intervals along this two-dimensional timeline.

I believe that the arts are a window into the past, the future, into the unknown, and into what's known. Inspiration is nothing more than insight into what our past and future holds. I believe from the making of the pyramids to space travel and all things in between, we move forward learning from our past.

I watch as little children instinctively know how to use a remote control that is not connected to the TV and accept it as normal, when in fact, I remember a time that we needed to get up to turn the TV off and on and change the channel; the remote control seemed magical.

I believe we can all tap into this knowledge if we so choose. I believe that I am here to learn, to experience, and to share. I believe that I am here to feel pain, love, and joy. I believe that I am here to reap wisdom from all of these experiences, to better understand human nature.

You may or may not believe in time travel. You may believe that these are the best of times or the worst of times. You may wonder what the meaning of life is. Or you may be amazed by all that surrounds us in nature and by human innovation. Either way, we move along the path of time whether we want to or not and experience time travel.

Chapter 6
Activism

Since my family situation became more hopeless, I turned my attention to finding hope in human rights protection for our transgender community. As trans activists, the first challenge we had was to endorse and try to pass Bill Siksay's private member's bill, Bill C-389, to amend the Canadian Human Rights Act and the Criminal Code (to add gender identity and gender expression). It was initially introduced in 2005, then again in 2009, and last introduced in the 40th Parliament, 3rd Session, which ended in March 2011 when an election was called. I and others like me were interviewed about our experiences of transgender discrimination, which made me feel like my suffering was not in vain. Unfortunately, because of the election, Bill C-389 was prorogued when it sat in the Senate and did not pass for the third time. Prorogued means any bills that have not passed into law when an election is called are automatically scrapped and need to be reintroduced by the newly elected government if they so choose.

I started getting involved with activism after March of 2007, when I had completed the Gender Journeys program at Sherbourne Health in Toronto. My activism started off very simply by going out and meeting people in the community and talking about what I had learned at Gender Journeys, various support groups, and human rights lobbying within Toronto and Ottawa. I left Gender Journeys feeling empowered with the knowledge and education I had received and began being an activist. I later gifted Rupert Raj, the head of Gender Journeys, a piece of art with a poem I'd written about the experience.

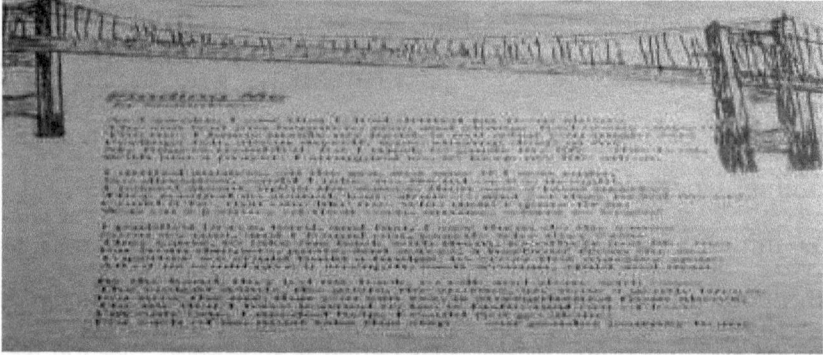

Gender Journey Poem (March 2007)

On June 26, 2009, the first official Trans March took place in Toronto, with more than 1,500 people in attendance. It coincided with the second time Bill Siksay's bill had been introduced into the federal Parliament and was inspired by similar marches in the USA.

The first-ever Toronto Trans March was organized by Karah Mathiason and her wife, Diane Grant. The march began in the hopes of creating "a safe place where everybody's welcome to be who they are" and immediately drew media attention. The March started at Bloor and Church Street on June 26, 2009, headed south and then dissolved into the crowd at Church and Wellesley, the main intersection in Toronto's gay village. It didn't end the way we hoped it would—we all got lost in the Pride revellers—but we had officially had our first Trans March in Toronto.

Stefonknee Wolscht at first Toronto Trans March (June 26, 2009)

In the fall and winter of 2009–10, a group of trans activists through Rainbow Health Ontario started the Trans Pulse Survey and set their sights on getting a census from 3,000 trans people who were over the age of fourteen to gather Canadian statistics on trans people and depression and suicide for use in teaching sensitivity training for public sector workers.

The official definition of 'gender identity' and 'gender expression,' as described by the Canadian government...

Gender Identity

Gender identity is each person's internal and individual experience of gender. It is their sense of being a woman, a man, both, neither, or anywhere along the gender spectrum.

A person's gender identity may be the same as or different from the gender typically associated with their sex assigned at birth. When a person's gender identity is different from the gender typically associated with their sex assigned at birth, this is often described as transgender or simply trans.

Gender identity is not the same as a person's sexual orientation.

Gender Expression

Gender expression is the way in which people publicly present their gender. It is the presentation of gender through such aspects as dress, hair, makeup, body language, and voice.

Next, I joined the Trans Lobby group and we worked with Queer Ontario and moved MPP Cheri DiNovo's Bill 33, "Toby's Act," through the Ontario legislature. The act was named in memory of the trans musician Toby Dancer, the music director at DiNovo's

Emmanuel Howard Park United Church. With the support of Cheri DiNovo, Glen Murray MPP, and activists Andrea Houston and Georgina Bencsik, as well as a large contingent from MCC Toronto and the Trans Lobby Group, plus members of the transgender community, we were able to lobby the Ontario government with facts and statistics gathered throughout Ontario from the Trans Pulse Survey (April 2010).

On June 22, 2010, we participated in the gender justice march at the G8/G20 Summit protests in Toronto, chanting things like "We're queer, we're fabulous, we're against the G20," and "My gender is not illegal." Marchers were fighting for women's and transgender rights.

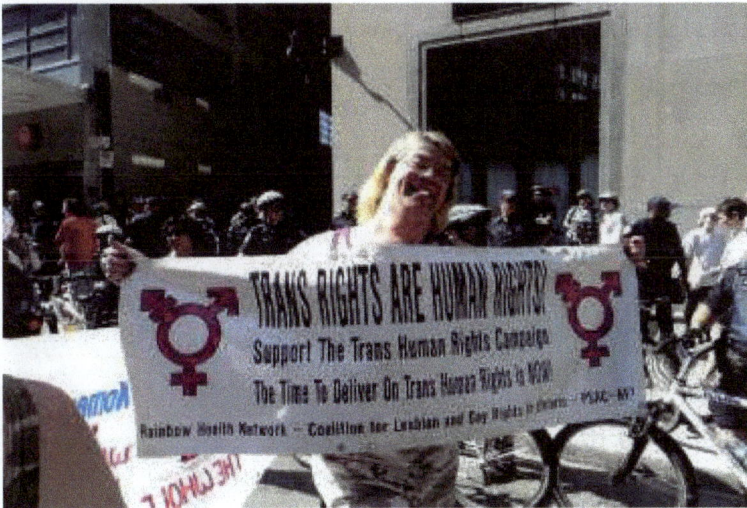

Leading the Gender Justice March (June 22, 2010)

Stefonknee Wolscht

On July 1, 2011, I organized and led the very first Toronto Trans March down Yonge Street, which was also the first time that I had organized an LGBTQ event. Pride Toronto told me that we were not allowed to go down Yonge as they had arranged for us to march down Church Street again, like we had done before and which ended in a fiasco, so I vowed that we would take over Yonge Street, like the Dyke March and the Pride Parade. With the support of Tom Decker of the Toronto Police Service, we travelled down from Norman Jewison Park at Gloucester and Yonge, down Yonge to Carlton, then to Allan Gardens, with me leading the way beside my truck. All along the route, we blared Lily Allen's song "Fuck You" on my sound system, dedicating it to various trans haters throughout Canada. The other half of the Trans March headed towards Church Street and both marches ended up meeting at Allan Gardens, which, from the air, looked like a huge heart surrounding the Gay Village.

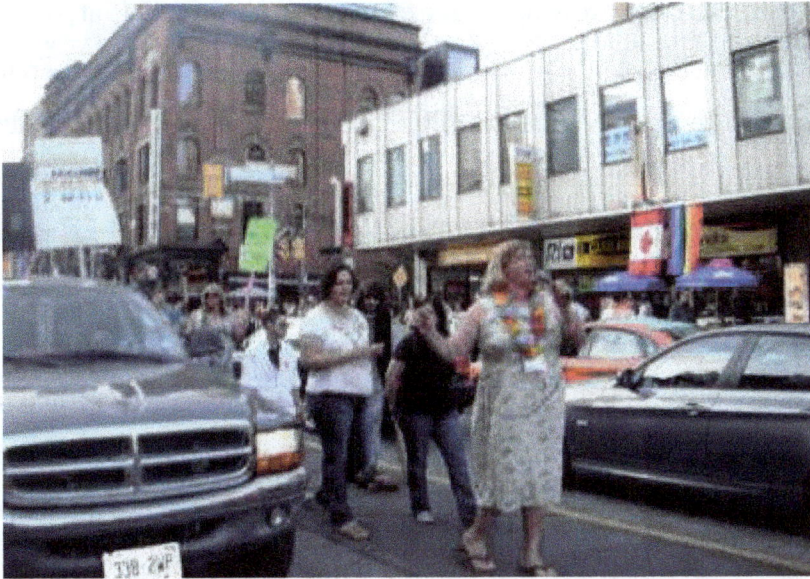

Shadmith and Chrystal Manzo, with Stefonknee leading the first Trans March down Yonge St. (July 1, 2011)

Organizing various marches in Toronto helped draw attention to our plight and finally, Bill 33, Toby's Act, was passed, despite three previous attempts over the years that had failed. On June 19, 2012, Toby's Law received royal assent, giving us trans rights and protection from discrimination throughout Ontario.

In June of 2013, the Toronto Trans March organized by Melissa Hudson and Nicki Ward ended up being not only the largest Trans March in Canada, but it was also recorded as the largest Trans March in the world. By this time, Pride Toronto knew we were serious about organizing these community-led transgender events, which were only growing larger every year, so in 2014, at World Pride in Toronto, they officially added the Yonge Street Trans March to the *Pride Guide*. In 2023, 10,000 marchers participated and one of the loudest groups at the June 23 Trans March was the contingent from Women's College Hospital, the first hospital in Toronto to provide transition-related surgical care to transgender and gender-diverse people.

We continued our fight and lobbied the federal government to add gender identity and gender expression to the Canadian Charter of Rights through Bill C-16. On May 17, 2016, Bill C-16 was introduced by the Minister of Justice, the Honourable Jody Wilson-Raybould.

Senator Donald Plett went out of his way to make this bill about using washrooms. He argued that if this were passed into law, then men would be given access to safe women's spaces, and predators would be allowed to enter into women's washrooms or women's shelters for illegal and perverted purposes. People opposed to Bill C-16 would soon call it "The Bathroom Bill."

On a trip to Ottawa in 2015 with Adrian Field, I went to visit Donald Plett at his office, and he was furious with me for tweeting that his wife "Betty should feed her baby," a common slur I used because I'd grown tired of his constant whining. Within minutes, he invited me up to his office, escorted by an RCMP officer for a ten-minute meeting, only to spend twenty minutes being yelled at for what I had written on Twitter. During his rant, he assured me that he could use male pronouns when talking about Amanda Ryan, a friend of mine who was an activist in Ottawa. I laughed at him and told him he was full of crap, that the "facts" that he was drumming up were all lies, and his opinion was not based on facts but rather on bad, right-wing religious rhetoric. I called him out on his transphobia and suggested that he back down because the movement to include trans rights was gaining momentum and his opinion was outdated, that he would eventually lose, and history would judge him for his lies.

The bill passed in the House of Commons by 248–40 votes and in the Senate by a vote of 67–11 with three abstentions. Bill C-16 received royal assent on June 19, 2017, and became law immediately.

Stefonknee in Ottawa to meet with Senator Donald Plett (March 26, 2015)

My Transgender Wolf

by Stefonknee Wolscht

Inspired by the Cherokee legend "The Wolves Within."

An old grandfather said to his grandson, who had come to him angry at a friend who had done an injustice to him, "Let me tell you a story. Once, I, too, felt a great hatred toward those who hurt me, with no regard for what they did. But I soon learned that hate only wears you down and does nothing to your enemy. It is like taking poison and expecting your enemy to die. I, too, have struggled with these feelings many times."

He continued, "It is as if there are two wolves inside me. One is good and does no harm. She lives in harmony with all around her, and she does not take offence when no offence was intended. She will only fight when it is right to do so, and in the right way. But the other wolf, ah! She is full of hate. The smallest thing will set her off into a fit of anger. She fights everyone, all the time, for no reason. She cannot think because her anger and hate are so great. It is helpless anger, for her anger will change nothing. Sometimes, it is hard to live with these two wolves inside me, for both of them try to control my spirit."

The boy looked intently into his grandfather's eyes and after much consideration, asked, "Which wolf wins, Grandfather?"

The Grandfather smiled and whispered, "The one I feed."

Contemplating this legend, I wondered how a trans person or Two-Spirit person could relate to this story.

I believe a Two-spirit person has one wolf, not two within themselves and their wolf exists for good, seeking out and destroying evil. She is not fed by what I think, say, or do. Rather, she is fed by what others think of transgendered people like me.

Every day, she watches and listens to the people I interact with—friends, family, strangers on the bus or in a mall, service providers, church communities, politicians, the justice system, and even me. Every day, I live in fear of being devoured by her. I worry that while she roams about seeking out injustice and evil, she hears and begins to believe the accusations and lies perpetuated against transgendered people like me. It is then that I am at my weakest. It is then that I cannot keep my focus on making my world a better place. It is then that I become afraid of being alone with myself, because it is then that the wolf within me transfers all the hatred of the world upon me and she seeks to destroy the very spirit that keeps her alive.

It is more than ironic that the early Christian explorers sought out and killed two-spirit members of North American First Nations by feeding them to war dogs. Four hundred years ago, public perception influenced the treatment of trans persons through fear and prejudice to clear the way to perpetuate their oppressive injustices against a culture they perceived as savages.

Hopefully, one day, we will live in a world where everyone seeks to cohabit in peace and love.

Chapter 7
Street Haven at the Crossroads

Moving into a shelter is quite the experience. Never having been homeless, always having lived in a house with family or friends, living in a shelter with strangers and strange rules was quite an adjustment for me. I remember thinking to myself that I didn't know how to be homeless; they don't teach this in school. I've already spoken about my days at Women's Residence. While I was there, I was given $4 a day PNA (Personal Needs Allowance) and two TTC tokens as well. I quickly saved up my $28 per week and my fourteen tokens to cash in and buy native cigarettes (tax-free cigarettes sold by First Nations). I had this hustle where I would sell the women in the shelter three cigarettes for one TTC token and if they needed to go somewhere on the bus or streetcar, I would lend them a Metropass. I would take all the tokens that I collected with me to speaking engagements throughout the city. I had a university professor, Pascal Murphy, who invited me to speak to his class about my homeless situation; he would buy my tokens and announce to his classes that I had these tokens for sale. On my best night, I sold seventy-five tokens and in my best week, I traded two hundred cigarettes. Except for the smell of the fresh cigarettes, this was a very good business. I would sit at my computer in the hallway between our bedrooms and the smoking balcony to provide women with cigarettes or a lighter. It was a very lucrative business and with the money I made, I could afford the transit fare to get to court. That went on for most of the time that I was at Women's Residence until I moved to Street Haven on September 23, 2009.

On Monday, September 21, after a doctor's appointment, I rang the bell on Street Haven's blue front door and asked if they had any beds. The social worker who opened the door, Bianca, was really excited to announce that they had just finished getting sensitivity training from The 519 in Toronto and that they would now start accepting trans women into the shelter. I would be their first trans woman. I was so happy, I would finally be in the shelter where they would accept me for who I was, and I would be close to my doctors at St. Mike's, my church, and Sherbourne Health. Despite being so depressed, I was desperate to move forward with my life, and I felt that I now had a place to live that would become like a home to me.

Street Haven at the Crossroads is an old three-story Victorian house in downtown Toronto, with two stories for the sheltered women and the top attic floor for administration. In front of the shelter was a massive elm tree that must have been 200 years old. It provided shade for the entire front lawn, but unfortunately, it has since been cut down.

When you buzzed the doorbell one of the staff would come and greet you to let you in. When they greeted you, they would be assessing if you were sober or stable enough to come into the shelter and not be disruptive. If you've never been in a shelter, the first thing you'd notice is that there is a well-structured routine incorporated into each day. The staff are there to make sure that everything runs smoothly.

Street Haven was always bustling with activity, from morning wake-up routine to going out into the city during the day to access public services or go to appointments. I found myself very busy throughout the week because of legal issues and support for my depression issues. We would leave the shelter around nine a.m. to go out into the city and return by about five p.m. when we would be allowed back inside again for supper. Sometimes, we'd be allowed to stay in if the weather was bad.

My days consisted of going to various appointments for counselling and heading to court or doctor's appointments for all my various ailments. Often there were times that I was away for a longer term in a hospital. Regardless of when we got home to the shelter, we would have dinner and do our chores, followed by watching the television in the living room. My favourite chore was doing the dishes. With thirty-five women in one house plus the staff, there were always coffee cups to wash, and plates were stacked by the dozens, plus all the pots and pans from cooking. They all needed to be washed, rinsed, and sterilized at least three times a day. Coffee cups were something I could wash all night long. I loved the sound of the dishes clanging in the hot water and the feeling of bubbles on my hands. Doing dishes at the shelter reminded me of the time I spent with my kids doing dishes at home.

In our bedrooms, we would often talk about our day's activities. I had a habit of sleeping with my doll, Franny, and my three little stuffed pigs, which I would sometimes lend out to other girls who were sad and depressed and needed something to snuggle with. We each had a twin bed and a tiny locker to hold our belongings, which usually consisted of a couple changes of clothes, our bathroom bag, and whatever valuables we might have. I had a laptop computer and a cell phone. I'd sleep with the key for my locker in my pillowcase.

We had a lot of time to kill in the evenings and one of our favourite things to do was playing euchre after dinner. We also had a patio set outside that was technically there for smokers, but everyone seemed to congregate outside when the weather was nice. I joined the women's choir because it was something fun to do and it also paid us $10 for volunteering to sing. We would go out into the community on occasion, doing small concerts to raise money for the shelter.

Street Haven Choir Concert (April 29, 2012)

There weren't too many social events other than people coming in to hold AA meetings, the choir, and on special holidays a family would come in and cook us a Thanksgiving or Christmas dinner. Once, we had a group of hairdressers come in and give us haircuts and manicures. They taught us to do makeup, which was a huge hit that had everyone in good spirits.

There are a lot of people in shelters who bring their personal baggage from trauma with them, and I was no exception; I would be struggling constantly with thoughts of suicide and depression from being isolated from my family. Some women came from broken homes like me, some came from abusive situations, some came from jail, and some just came because they'd had bad luck and lost everything. Having so many different personalities and so many different triggers in one building meant that sometimes, things could erupt into yelling. The staff were quick to come out and settle things down to bring peace into the house.

Book cover sketch by Stefonknee Wolscht for Street Haven
(October 20, 2010)

While I was at Street Haven, I became aware of the BDSM community in Toronto. I quickly learned that I love pain, I loved people telling me what to do, and I loved being hurt. I would float into a happy space if someone was beating me. I hated my life, I hated my body, and pain was my only release for the emotions that I could not deal with.

I met a lot of nice people who were Dommes and others who were submissive. BDSM is not necessarily about sex. A lot of people look at it as some kind of perversion, but in reality, it's a lot of kinky people getting together socializing and providing a consensual release for inner turmoil. A Domme named Vermilion Fire bought me my first doll, Franny. She didn't just buy me some nice things when I was homeless. She also helped me set up my banking. She gave me $800 to open an account so that I could actually take the money that I was paid from doing outreach for various groups to teach them about gender identity and the sensitivity around pronouns and keep it safe in the bank. Vermilion Fire was also very generous with the other women at the shelter. She would often take me shopping in a cute outfit to buy ice cream, chocolate, and candies for the women at the shelter. It was always a hit when we came back with shopping bags full of treats for everyone. She liked to keep me as her little girl, which allowed me to escape by being an eight-year-old girl for a short time. This was something that I was never allowed to do as a child.

I believe age play is an excellent way to deal with excessive stress and thoughts of suicide. When I escape into my "little" space and play with my dolls, colour, or do puzzles, I find that I lose track of time, and the stress that causes my depression vanishes. Vermilion Fire had a way of making me feel beautiful and helped me learn to love myself again. While I was under her protection, she would care for me when nobody else cared, she made me feel human when nobody else made me feel human, and she would beat me when I asked her to please help me release some of the pain that I felt inside. We would agree on a safe word that would be used to stop the beatings if I felt that it was going too far, but it never did. Those beatings would send me into a thing called 'subspace,' where I would see myself gliding over mountains and over castles with dragons. I would escape into this world of make-believe, where everything was fine. My mind was relieved of all the thoughts of suicide and all the things that were going wrong, especially the loss of my children and the pain that it caused me. Somehow, the physical pain let all the mental pain go free. Once, I had a session that left me in subspace for six days.

In the BDSM community, there are rules and there is respect for the Doms and Dommes as well as respect for the subs. Everything is consensual, and everything is discussed beforehand at meetings. A 'munch' is a vanilla or non-kinky meeting held at a venue where you can negotiate terms of engagement, and everything is predetermined before anyone engages in a session.

I know this may be upsetting to some people, but it was very normal for those of us in the community. BDSM activity was there for me when I needed it and it's still there if I want to have it, but at this point, I am able to get myself into "little space" on my own with my cat and my dolls and my teddy bears. In little space, everything is so much better.

I remember once at CAMH, I was on the women's floor, and I asked everyone to try to get a teddy bear for a play party that we would have in the common room. I arranged to have candies, cookies, juice boxes, some children's music, colouring books and puzzles, and yoga mats laid out so we could lie on the floor and play. On the night we had the play party, the nurses told us they'd never seen the ward so quiet and happy. I was glad that all the women trusted me and let themselves become little again to see how age play could help them cope with all their struggles. I hope someday they will study the benefits of age play for adults as a therapy for depression, suicidal thoughts, and anxiety.

Stefonknee during Play Date at CAMH (September 17, 2017)

This was a far cry from my stable life at home with my children, fixing cars and taking care of my family. I don't think you could get a more opposite world to live in than being in a shelter and using BDSM as a coping mechanism. It wasn't as good as being a mom to my kids, but it helped me in my time of pain and suffering.

A Homeless Christmas

While some might say that the homeless have chosen to live and survive outside of mainstream society, I suggest to you that it is mainstream society that dictates where and how the homeless live. In every society, there are those who seem different, different enough to be despised and spoken ill of, different enough to justify our indifference towards them since society perceives them to be less than whole.

Homeless, outcast, rejected ... lepers in a modern world that cannot dictate the rules of inclusion, rules of engagement, rules created by a majority used to suppress the rights of a minority. A person who is an outcast is left with little, if anything, to survive on, isolated from the "haves" in hopes that the elements or even evolution will deal with them and erase them from our thoughts and consciences. Once someone has been ostracized by the majority, it is near impossible for them to re-establish their status within society without the help of those with power and privilege. Like many species that isolate their weak, we as humans are somehow empowered whenever we ignore those who are different, leaving them to be devoured in isolation. At the same time, we find protection in numbers for ourselves.

What is it, then, that makes it so easy to dismiss the homeless when reminded of their suffering at this time of year? How do we celebrate with lavish spending and overeating while distracted from the reminders all around us that some still suffer? Is it the denial of our own vulnerability? Are we so afraid of being stripped of our rank, our status, left defenceless and naked? Any one of us could be next... like a target in a game of dodge ball, we relish someone else's misfortune, knowing deep inside that it could have been us.

Think of the vulnerable as canaries in a coal mine; they are the alarm bells ringing out, telling us that something is going drastically wrong. Society must take responsibility for putting them in harm's way. It is common to ask what the poor are doing with their lives or how they got themselves into such desperate circumstances, making them responsible for the situation they are in. It is our very social structure, our social status, that is precariously vulnerable and fragile, that pushes the poor to the bottom. Most middle- and lower-class Canadians are only a few paycheques away from poverty. If we were to consider the vast fortunes accumulated by the few who control the world's wealth and have done so throughout history by taking the lion's share for themselves off of the toil and sweat of the poor, we would see why the poor are with us. We never feel the need to ask the wealthy how they earned the right to draw dividends from our labour, or how they earned the right to control such fortunes… we do not hold them accountable for the poor. Rather, we beg and plead for them to be charitable and find it in their hearts to let us have their table scraps.

Perhaps God is watching us to see how or if we care for the canaries. Perhaps God is waiting until it is safe for the canaries before opening our eyes to "the light" in this filthy coal mine we call civilized society. God knows our hearts and our souls and is walking among us, walking with us. God is born into the world today in a lowly manger, surrounded by canaries that we call angels, away from the rich and powerful, waiting for peace on earth before letting us experience heaven on earth. Like the magi, find God, not in the bible story of Christmas long ago, but rather every day in the people and places of our world.

Stefonknee Wolscht

December 25, 2010.

Chapter 8
Public Speaking

On September 2, 2009, I was arrested. Yet, on October 3, a fantastic thing happened while I was riding a streetcar: I saw a sticker for the Women and Trans Collective at the University of Toronto on the back of the seat in front of me. I looked them up on the internet and phoned them immediately to see if it would be okay if an older person came to join them. They told me to come, and they gave me the times that they were open, so I went straight over. I met Michelle, a facilitator who welcomed me into the collective and gave me a tour of the centre, which included a library, a common area, and a kitchen. They were extremely trans-friendly, and I met a lot of transgender and trans allies in that group. I started to attend and continued going there for more than eight years. As a collective, we would decide what kind of activism needed to be done to draw attention to various marginalized people, including transgender people. We would attend marches for missing and murdered Indigenous women, march in the Toronto Pride parade, and advocate for transgender rights in Ontario through Toby's Bill. And sometimes, we would sit around on the couch and just hang out or write poetry or do some kind of craft, and we would make time to colour posters for some activism work. It was the beginning of my involvement with activism in the community. To be completely honest, my daughter Amanda was a student at U of T, and I hoped and prayed that I would bump into her one day while hanging out with kids who were the same age as her.

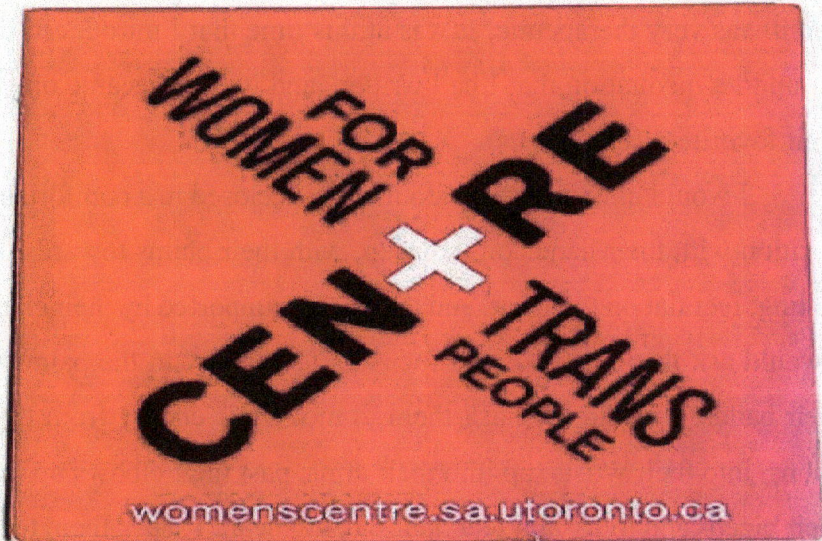

University of Toronto sticker that started my journey into public speaking (October 3, 2009)

The Women and Trans Collective, also known as the Centre for Women and Trans People, was a vibrant and busy group run by Margaret and Sabra at that time. They had resources in their library about LGBTQ+ stuff, including a section on trans history. They also had weekly luncheons where we prepared food and ate together with other members from the group. They were a very caring group of people who went out of their way to support marginalized people like me and make Toronto a better place for everyone.

I got to know a lot of young people who were my kids' age, and sitting there with my eyes closed I sometimes would imagine that I was back home again. Their bantering and laughter were nice, and it was very therapeutic. It was at this time that I introduced the group to a meditation that I had written, and it soon became one of their favorite meditations.

I would have them sit with their eyes closed in a comfortable position with their hands on their lap, with their palms towards the ceiling, feet flat on the floor, and their body supported by their chair. I would ask them to relax and focus on the energy in the palms of their hands. I would then ask them to move this energy from their palms, into their wrists, up into their arms, past their elbows up into their biceps and to try and feel their pulsing heart. I'd ask them to be aware of the inner workings of their body, the life-giving pulse that has happened every second of every hour of every day since they were conceived. I would remind them that all is well, and all is well, in all manner of things, all is well. Everything is exactly as it should be, and their heart is beating to keep their body nourished and healthy, just as they had when they were floating inside their mother's womb, their cells multiplying and creating the unique person that they were to be. Everything that they needed was contained inside their mother and all was well, and all is well, in all manner of things, always well.

With the beating of their heart, beating with the rhythm of the waves and like the tides on the ocean that come in and out by the gravity of the Moon as the world spins, all is well. The Moon and the Earth are orbiting the Sun with all the other planets, and all is well, and all is well, in all manner of things, all is well. I would then ask them to push this energy up through their shoulders and through their neck up to the back of their skull and to feel this energy as it rises up at the back of their brain over the top of their head and down behind their eyebrows and eyes, just above their sinuses and to allow the stress of the day to evaporate. They would then multiply this energy by pushing more and more good energy up into their brain and accumulating it to the point where I would count down three, two, one. They would release the energy out through their body, out their arms and out their legs and hands and feet into the universe.

Their energy would move up through the ceiling and out into the sky, up into the upper atmosphere and out into outer space, where they would feel the weightlessness of zero gravity. I allowed them to drift off to a faraway planet past the Moon, past all of Earth's orbit and into the Milky Way. I would jokingly have them sit on the Milky Way and take a bite out of it to see if it tasted like the chocolate bar. Then I would have them dive back down towards Earth, coming in closer and closer to the blue planet that we call home, past the moon, and dive through the upper atmosphere and descend down through the clouds and into the ocean.

I would have them splash into the ocean and be carried away on the back of a dolphin that would take them down to the bottom of the ocean, where they would see a surreal world, very different from what we witness on the surface. A world where fish move freely around in zero gravity, plants of every colour, size, and texture surround us and the soft sand beneath us is warm as we lie there on the bottom of the ocean, staring at the silvery surface of the water above.

I would ask them to relax and feel the energy and know that all is well, and all is well, in all manner of things, all is well. As the Earth orbits with the moon around the Sun, with all the other planets together in our universe, as they've done for millennia, all is well.

I would then have the dolphin pick them up, take them up to the silvery surface of the water and deposit them onto the warm sand of a beach. They would lie there and feel the tide come in and touch their toes because of the gravity of the moon, and all is well. They would then feel their spirit lift up into the air and come back to the school, come down through the roof back into the room and back into their bodies. They could feel the energy in the palms of their hands and in their arms and in the back of their neck and around their skull and know that all is well, and all is well, in all manner of things, all is well. When they were ready, they would open their eyes, refreshed and ready to share in the day's activities.

Because of my connection with the Centre for Women and Trans People, I was soon invited to speak about my ordeals to students in various courses at the University of Toronto. I enjoyed standing in front of a large group in a lecture hall, sharing with them what I was going through. I would acknowledge the privilege that I had, having been born white and male, and how I had lost that privilege when I transitioned to become female. I would share with them all the benefits that I had up until age forty-six, things that I thought I had earned because of my hard work, and how that year I had lost it all and so much had changed in my life. I was now dealing with mental health issues, I was now a homeless person, and now I had a criminal record as well. But in reality, I was still the same person I was before except now I was presenting as female.

It was really nice to be able to contribute to the group at the centre and be welcomed as often as I wished. I went there when I was having a great day, and I went when there was nothing to cheer about, but they always welcomed me and helped me find a safe space to be myself, to deal with whatever I had to deal with. I made many friends who would then go on to graduate and start lives of their own, and I encouraged them to remember the meditation and draw from it whenever they felt they needed to centre themselves and get grounded.

Also at this time, Tanya Gallagher and Pascal Murphy invited me to come and speak about my ordeal at Ryerson University, now known as Toronto Metropolitan University. In their Homeless in Society class, I was at my highest anxiety level. Still, I accepted the invitation and I found it to be very therapeutic because it meant that I wasn't suffering in a vacuum.

I would start my talk by introducing myself and explaining to people what the difference was between 'sex' and 'gender'; I would say that gender was something between your ears that identifies who you are as a person, and sex was something assigned at birth because of what was between your legs. Then I suggest that being transgender is very similar to wearing your shoes on the wrong feet—they're the right shoes and they're your shoes, but something doesn't feel right. Given a chance, you would probably remove the shoes and put them on the opposite feet, making them feel much more comfortable. Being transgender is like feeling uncomfortable in your own skin and taking every opportunity to express yourself as the person you feel yourself to be. Then I would start my talk, which went like this…

"Hello, my name is Stefonknee Wolscht, and I would like to share my story with you so that you might better understand why transgender persons need to have explicit protection within the Canadian Charter of Rights. I was born on June 24, 1963, as Paul Andrew Wolscht in Scarborough, Ontario and raised on a farm in

Mount Albert. By age six, I remember seeing men wearing dresses on our black and white television; it was the Stonewall Riots, in 1969. I knew that I identified with these people as I, too, wanted to be a girl.

"I struggled with this secret most of my life and seemed to know at a young age that it should be hidden from the world. By 1984, my girlfriend found out that I needed to dress and express myself as a girl and she accepted me despite my gender issues. In 1986, we married, and we had seven beautiful children in a large but otherwise average family, fully participating in our community and our Catholic church."

By this point, I would be shaking and crying, but I carried on.

"Having been raised on a family farm inspired me to run my auto repair business from home so I could actively participate in raising our children. My wife continued her education and soon became a teacher, later a principal, and we prospered, blessed by God with healthy children, and loving family and friends. We led a normal life, working hard, raising children and grandchildren, volunteering, going to church etc. We were just another middle-class family trying to survive in a modern, busy world. In March 2007, I attended Gender Journeys, a support group at Sherbourne Health in Toronto and began to better understand my gender issues. At this time, I realized that we, as a family, needed help. I suggested we get counselling, but my wife refused, stating that she wouldn't let those downtown doctors ram their gay agenda down our kids' throats. By May 2009, she requested that I stop being transgender or move out, meaning I abandon my family, my home, and my business, and start my life over again ..."

... and you know the rest of this story.

I used my experiences to educate people about trans rights and transphobia and the reason why we needed sensitivity training and human rights protection throughout Canada.

Things were changing for me. Kyle Scanlon at The 519 hired and trained me to do sensitivity training. Trainers from The 519 would be sent to various groups, including The Centre for Women and Trans Collective, to teach people about pronouns and transgender issues and ways to make trans people feel included in their programs. It paid pretty well. I worked with a team of people, and we usually went out in groups of two or three, so we had a chance to socialize. It was very triggering to go through some of the hard questions they would ask to justify getting respect as a trans person. Some people would question why we needed any rights at all. Those were few and far between, but they still stung and triggered us.

I worked for The 519 until June of 2012. On the Friday before Pride, I'd done a workshop at George Brown College with my manager, Kyle Scanlon, and it hadn't gone well. After we left, I asked him if he needed to go to the hospital with me, but he told me he was okay. I took myself to St. Mike's Hospital because I'd been triggered, and I didn't feel safe to go home.

I left the hospital the following Thursday on a day pass, to go do a job for The 519. When I got to the office, everything on Kyle's desk was the way we had left it prior to the George Brown seminar, and nothing was ready for the workshop that day. This was unlike Kyle: he was always organized and if he didn't have something ready, he would message me and let me know that he needed my help to get something together. I never got a call.

I did the workshop and when I returned the information folder to the office, I mentioned to the staff that something was wrong with Kyle. They brushed me off and I didn't think any more of it. But the next day, I came back to the office, and everything was still exactly as it was left the night before, so I told the other supervisor that if they didn't check Kyle's apartment, I would call 911 and have the police go in and check on him.

I would later find out that when he got home from the workshop at George Brown College, he had taken his life.

Talking about these issues that we experienced could be very traumatic and would often leave us vulnerable to self-harm. We had asked The 519 to give us access to some mental health supports to help us deal with the triggers. Our efforts were in vain. Even with Kyle's death, nothing was changed with regard to getting us mental health support. That would be the last workshop that I did, and I chose self-care over public education.

In 2010, one of the students from Ryerson did a documentary about me called *Living Two Lives, Dying a Thousand Deaths*. Dana Greenbaum did a great job of taking stock of those early years of homelessness, mental health challenges, and incarceration. I've posted the video on my YouTube channel so that my children can see what I was going through and perhaps reach out to me.

I continued with my advocacy for our community and am happy to say that on June 19, 2012, Toby's Law passed the Legislature and protected trans people from discrimination because of Gender Identity or Gender Expression under the Ontario Charter of Rights.

Through the work of my friends Cheri DiNovo, Andrea Houston, Martine Stonehouse, Susan Gapka, Georgina Bencsik, Davina Hader, and myself, we succeeded in making it illegal for people to discriminate against trans women and men in Ontario.

It took a few more years but by June 19, 2017, the Canadian federal government added Gender Identity and Gender Expression to the Canadian Charter of Rights and Freedoms.

Although this was great news, it's too bad that Kyle Scanlon wasn't alive to witness these momentous occasions. Kyle was a really nice guy, very good at his job but also very vulnerable, like me, to triggers, and unfortunately, that last workshop was too much for him to handle. I miss you, Kyle, and I hope you're in a better place watching down over us.

Chapter 9
Joubert House/Religion

After living in the residence at Street Haven for about three months, I was asked if I wanted to go into transitional housing, which was right next door in another Victorian house. Knowing that I would have a room to myself, with a key, and I wouldn't be forced to go out in all sorts of weather during the day, which was nice because of the damage done to my heart, I immediately accepted the offer.

At Joubert House, there were five women in the entire house, and I shared my kitchen and bathroom with one neighbour, Amy, on the top floor. We had a recreation room in the basement with a television and a kettle to make tea. I would spend countless hours with my housemate, Joan, talking about my adventures and watching television as we sipped tea and became really good friends.

Having a room that was my own was so nice, and having a place with such great people gave me hope. My prayers had been answered because having a home like Street Haven, and Joubert House, proved to be a gift from God to help me while I was struggling with my depression. Going to a Catholic hospital like St.

Michael's in Toronto also provided me with opportunities to go to the Chapel and to thank God for protecting me from myself.

Although I continued to go to the Catholic church, by the end of 2009, I found the Metropolitan Community Church of Toronto (MCCT), an LGBT church in Toronto. I guess this would be a good time to share with you my spirituality and my religious affiliations.

I was baptized Roman Catholic in 1963 and was raised in a Catholic home where we went to church every Sunday. I didn't ask to be born into a Catholic family, and neither did I choose to be baptized Roman Catholic, but I was, so here we go. I took my faith seriously from a young age and I often asked God why I was made this way, made a girl trapped inside of a boy's body. Other than that, I was your normal, average Christian kid.

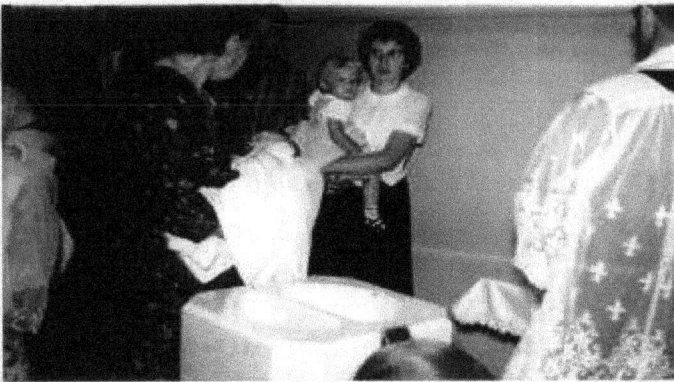

Baptism for Paul Jr. held by my Oma Heming. Monica held by my mom. (July 28, 1972)

In 1969, I took my first communion. I gave my life to Jesus, giving thanks to God for our meals, thanking God for our friends and family, and praying for our friends in distress, which included praying for myself before tests and exams, asking the Holy Spirit to give me clarity of mind. Again, wearing a boy's suit to my first communion instead of a pretty white dress bothered me, but I didn't let that stop me from making a commitment to God.

Paul Wolscht Jr. First Holy Communion, St. John Chrysostom, Newmarket (May 14, 1972)

God and I would get along pretty well for all of my life, me saying thank you when there was something to give thanks for and yelling and swearing at God when I felt frustrated and trapped with the choices I was given in my life. Needless to say, I had to go to confession a lot because I swore a lot, I was mad at God a lot, and I was putting on girl's dresses all the time, believing myself to be a girl, which was also considered a sin in the Catholic church.

L to R: Eric, Paul, Michael, Robert, and Monica Wolscht leaving for Church (May 14, 1972)

Jesus, God, and the Holy Spirit seemed to listen to me whether I was wearing pants or a dress, so in my mind, it was okay to be transgender even though I didn't know the word at the time. Having a Catholic girlfriend who participated in my cross-dressing also helped alleviate some of the guilt; after all, why would God find this woman to be with me, who was totally accepting of my cross-dressing, if I was such a bad sinner?

169

I didn't go to a Catholic school because we lived in Mount Albert, a small town that had only one public school and it was too far for my parents to drive us to get to the Catholic school in Sharon, Ontario. Later, I went to a public high school in Newmarket, Huron Heights Secondary School. My only formal theological teaching came from Iris Reddy at Sunday school, as a child preparing for my first communion, and from Sunday sermons listening to the priest.

When I was in grade ten, I heard about this group that met outside of church, a group for young people to learn about God. It started with a retreat called COR (Christ in Others Retreat) weekend. Something happened to me on my first COR weekend that opened my heart up to Jesus. I really felt connected to the church for the first time in my life. It was no longer just a relationship between me and God. I now felt like an active participant in the church, despite having spent my youth as an altar server at Our Lady of Good Counsel church in the town of Sharon. While I was growing closer to God, my dad was distancing himself from God. My mom came on the Sunday afternoon to pick me up from COR in tears. She told me that my father was unbearable that weekend; it seemed like the closer I got to Jesus, the angrier he would get, and this was the worst she'd ever seen him. I felt so sorry for my mom having to suffer like that, but she appreciated the fact that I found a relationship with God and Jesus that was more than just your average going-to church thing we were doing. My mom and I never talked about the details of what happened; she was just glad it was over, and she knew something special had happened to me because of the way my dad reacted.

Maria never did the COR weekend; it was too churchy for her, which I regretted because I think she would have made some good friends who would have helped her deal with problems like my cross-dressing. On the other hand, I embraced everything about the life I now chose to live as a teenager. My faith grew stronger. I started attending events with youth in the Catholic school system and strengthened my bond with the church. I kept going to COR events up until I got married.

As a Catholic father, I loved taking my family to church and participating in the service as a Eucharistic minister and later as a Reader. One day, my daughter asked me why we had to go to church. I told her, "You don't have to go to church. You know what time our van leaves, and if you are in the van then you're coming with us. If you're not, you can stay home." None of my kids stayed home. They all had a relationship with God and were very active in church life, including our participation in Youth-to-Youth ministry events in Montrose, Michigan and in the Knights of Columbus.

When my two oldest daughters were ready to make their confirmation, I inquired as to the possibility of doing my confirmation with them because I had never done it as a teenager. I was so active with the youth that everyone thought I'd done my confirmation, but remember, I was going to a public school.

We took catechism classes in Newmarket because my kids were no longer in the Catholic school system. They went to Pickering College, which was a private Quaker school. Mrs. Iris Reddy was our catechism teacher and ironically, she was also the Sunday school teacher that I had when I took my first communion back in 1972. Here we were, sitting in a classroom thirty years later with the same teacher who brought me to God in the first place.

I ran into a hitch during my catechism registration in that I didn't have my first communion certificate. Still, I had a picture of myself coming out of the church with my first communion ribbon on my left sleeve, which she took as proof. When she investigated, she ended up finding my certificate still on file at the church because they didn't know where to mail it. Ironically, I was never given my confirmation certificate and I still don't have it to this day; so much for the archives of the Catholic Church.

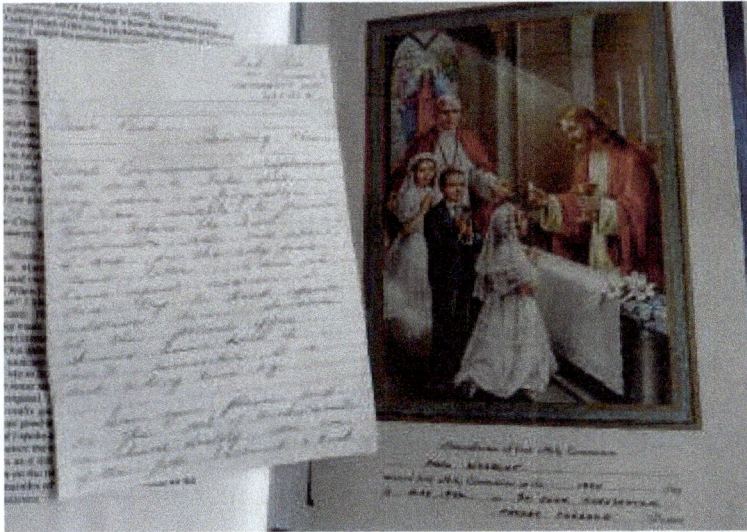

February 2, 2004: Received First Holy Communion diploma after my Confirmation with Chavonne and Amanda in the fall of 2003

The letter attached read,

"Dear Paul, Sending this First Communion Diploma at such a late date may seem unforgivable. I was unable to procure them before the First Communion date and when I did in the city sometime later, I did not have your address. I did try to track your address down. Someone at the parish office should have had it. I can't remember, it's such a long time ago. Can you please send me the audio cassettes on Church History? One of the girls borrowed a book… Mrs. Reddy:" She was such a great woman. May she rest in peace.

Our confirmation went beautifully. It was an honour to do it with my two daughters and a beautiful way to receive the sacrament. After my confirmation, my faith grew exponentially stronger, and I found myself talking to God all the time. By 2003, God started talking back to me.

Okay, okay, I know what you're thinking. The doctors at the hospital would always ask me if I heard voices and I told them, "You're not going to like this, but I really do. God talks to me." So, stop laughing and try to focus on where I'm going here—it sounds unbelievable, but I promise this really happened.

April 6, 2003, at four a.m., was the first time I was awoken by God's voice in a dream. I was to go to the computer and sit down and type out what I had been told. I was told to "go to the front of the church and tell the congregation to say goodbye to Fr. Christopher Walsh and thank him for praying for them." It was a Sunday morning. So, I went to the front of the church, and I said those words and the following Friday, he passed away. It was the last Sunday he was alive. So, tell me, would you still think of me as crazy?

Anyway, in that dream, God told me that Fr. Chris had done a lot of amazing things in his life, and I was given details of his missionary work in China during World War II. I was watching it like a movie, and when I recited what I had seen to Fr. Chris, he was shocked because, in my vision, I saw him consecrating the host and the wine to St. Joseph, not to God. Father Christopher had secretly consecrated his life to St. Joseph and every time he raised the Eucharist or the chalice, he would replace God with St. Joseph in his mind. He did this silently in front of the congregation. He never told a living soul that he had done this, but I told him God knew, and God was okay with it.

So, needless to say, I started taking my conversations with God very seriously and quite often, God would give me information that I needed to know. I've already shared with you that God talked to me at St. Mike's Hospital where he told me to help the patient in the next room beside mine, Angela.

God also told me things about other patients on the floor that I could not have known, but my nurse Tatiana kept a copy of the list that I made in my chart, that I was prophesying. She would later have them reassess the diagnosis of my being delusional.

Another interesting thing that happened while God was talking to me is people nearby could feel a really addictive sensation of weightlessness as if floating on your feet or on a chair. Both my children and friends felt these feelings, which they really were addicted to, and they loved to be around me whenever God was talking to me.

This started in 2003 and is still with me to this day, so I do believe that being transgender, or two-spirit, as the First Nations people call it, gives us the ability to hear and understand things that others don't hear and see. In many of the First Nations cultures, the "Shaman" identified as two-spirit, has this role in the community.

One such incident happened while I was at Joubert House. I was told to go to Moss Park to help a friend, Esther. When I got to the park, I saw Esther beside a tree covered in blood. She had exchanged sex for drugs and the drug dealer had really hurt her. I took Esther to St. Mike's hospital, and we sat there in the waiting room with her stoned and covered in blood. I was really saddened by the way she was treated by the staff at the hospital, so I asked if I could have some water and a washcloth to wash her off so they could see that she was just like any other person. Esther was a really nice friend who would do anything for anyone at the shelter. She would often just start cleaning the entire dining room and kitchen by herself; she loved to stay busy and help out. To see her like this broke my heart. I cleaned her up and I asked the hospital if they could hold her overnight because she couldn't return to the shelter in that state. She had been using drugs and Street Haven forced women to practice abstinence from drugs and alcohol while at the shelter. Esther needed a place to sleep it off and I asked if she could do it there and I would be back in the morning to pick her up. They were reluctant to let her stay, but they got her a bed in Rotary, a place in the hospital where homeless people could get a good night's sleep. When I came to pick her up in the morning, her belongings were all gone but she was safe and sober. I brought her back to the shelter and she was allowed to have a bed. It's times like this that I realize God puts me in places where I can try and do some good.

While living at Joubert House, I continued attending Sunday services at Our Lady of Lourdes, the Catholic church in my neighborhood, until I found it difficult to go to church as a Catholic trans woman because they wouldn't let me volunteer and be part of the church community. It was at this time that I found a new spiritual home at MCCT.

MCCT had held the very first gay marriage anywhere in the world just prior to my coming to join their congregation. I started going there because they were the LGBT church in my neighbourhood, and I'd stumbled across them during the summer of 2009 when I saw a church congregation at the Pride events, holding a Christian service called Church on Church. For a while, I continued going to Our Lady of Lourdes Catholic Church and MCCT at the same time, but I was getting a lot more out of my participation at MCCT. Sitting through the service was very difficult at times because it would remind me of going to church with my children. But the music at MCCT was the nicest music I could have had to cry to; our choir is unbelievable. I made many friends at my new church, and they helped support me through the rough times. They would invite me to go up for a blessing on Mother's Day, and they respected my gender identity and always called me Stefonknee.

At MCCT, I met really great clergy and deacons. One in particular, Linda Leenders, went out of her way to help counsel me on being shunned by my family and the loss of my children. Linda spent countless hours working with different therapeutic modes in an attempt to get rid of the suicidal thoughts. She even went so far as to call my daughter Nicole to try to set up a meeting to bring her back into my life, but Nicole wasn't ready yet. Linda took care of me when I couldn't take care of myself. She prayed for me, she would invite me to her house, and we would spend countless hours talking about my family life and ways for me to move on and try to love living again. Ironically, Linda is also the person who helped edit this book and encouraged me to finish it and tell my story to the world.

In 2018, I had a mental breakdown at MCCT. While I attempted to serve a parishioner the Eucharist, my jaw started to shake, I was crying, and I couldn't put the Eucharist into his mouth. I just couldn't do it. Everything felt hopeless. Shortly after that, I stopped going to church completely and stayed home on Sundays for the next five years.

It was at this point that my doctor suggested I see a psychiatrist by the name of Dr. Shapiro. Dr. Shapiro had a practice where he mentored five interns, and he asked me if it was okay if they sat in on our sessions. I agreed, not knowing what it would be like to share my innermost fears with six strangers, but I needed something to help me through this tough time and I didn't have any money to pay for therapy myself.

At our first appointment, I was sitting on the couch looking at the six of them staring back at me, when Dr. Shapiro asked, "Are you feeling suicidal right now?"

To which I responded, "I wasn't, until you asked me the question, and now I am. I just realized that I'm up on the tenth floor, and if I were to jump out the window, I would definitely end my life."

Dr. Shapiro responded by saying that he would have to clean up the mess.

I refuted that by saying, "Someone from the city would have to clean up the mess on the sidewalk."

Dr. Shapiro wasn't amused, but he then went to each of the interns and asked them how that made them feel? They each responded with something to the effect of it being sad and that I really needed help. We chatted for a while about my mood and whether or not it was safe for me to go home, to which I responded that I was not in crisis and I was sure by the time I reached the ground level, I would be safe.

After that session, I was feeling suicidal one night and ended up calling the police crisis line and asking for a crisis team to come and talk to me. I was hoping to talk to a crisis nurse to sort things out in my head. Unfortunately, four police officers knocked on my door and they immediately handcuffed me and led me to their cruiser. and I was escorted to CAMH and immediately formed and kept there in the crisis unit.

I recognized one of the doctors at CAMH as one of the interns who worked with Dr. Shapiro, and I assured him that I was not suicidal. I was just really depressed. I asked if he could have me discharged so that I could go back to see Dr Shapiro next Thursday. Unfortunately, he was unable to get me discharged. On the afternoon of the Wednesday prior to my appointment with Dr. Shapiro, I told the doctor on call that I was not suicidal and that I was prepared to call a lawyer to secure my release. I called a lawyer, and I told her that I was being held there on a form despite my not being suicidal. She asked me the questions that everyone asked, *Are you suicidal? Do you have a plan? And are you okay to go home?* I answered no, no, and yes. It was at that moment that the doctor signed the papers to have me discharged.

The next day, at Dr. Shapiro's office, I told him that I was lucky to be there because I was being held against my will at CAMH. His only concern was who would pay the $120 that he couldn't charge OHIP if I missed my appointment. I suggested that I had lost five days of my life and was not compensated and that I'm sure he'd be okay missing one hour's pay. I got up frustrated and was ready to leave when he asked me if he should pencil me in for the next week.

I told him to do whatever he wanted to do, but I would not be coming back. I did not appreciate the way he talked to me. The next morning, I got a call from one of the interns, inviting me to come to his office at Toronto Western Hospital to talk about what had happened the night before. He was upset and crying, and he felt like he was helpless to stop that from happening to me. I assured him that it was not his fault and that I would be better off not going to those appointments and getting triggered. I would have many more suicide attempts throughout the next two years.

On the evening of February 28, 2010, I was heading home from a talk at U of T. I was riding the Dundas streetcar towards home, and I had to cross Yonge Street. Unfortunately, the Canadian men's hockey team won Olympic gold in Vancouver that day. The bars had let out and people were celebrating in the street with open bottles of alcohol. When our streetcar arrived at Yonge Street, it couldn't proceed any further. The doors opened and the driver said we'd have to walk from there. So here I was, walking through this crowd of drunken men celebrating the win.

While passing through the intersection, a group of five men started following me as I wore a dress. They would hurl insults at me, stick their face over my shoulder and threaten me as I walked with my friend Amy back to Joubert House. When we got to Church and Dundas, I decided to let Amy go home with my purse, my earrings, and my cell phone, and I would deal with these five guys

181

before they found out where we lived. I turned to the biggest guy right there under the bright lights of the intersection and said, "I guess you and I are going to dance and then your friends are going to kill me?" I then approached him ready to do battle.

At this point, they all backed off and said, "Whoa, who said anything about fighting?"

I said, "Oh, so those are all just empty threats?" and I turned around to leave and they went back in their own direction. I was not attacked that night, but knowing they were drunk, I had my concerns. Sometimes, it pays to stand up to your bullies.

In January 2023, I started going back to MCCT every Sunday again. I renewed my connection with my church friends and even became a member this year after years of attending without being a member. It's nice to know that there are people who patiently wait while I get my act together.

A few times, I brought the women from Joubert House with me to church to celebrate our humanity. I also brought women from the shelter to help cook meals at Christmas and Thanksgiving. MCC Toronto prioritized having a special day for those who were spending the holidays alone and would serve a full meal with turkey and all the trimmings, and desserts to anyone who wanted to come. Those of us from the shelter were amazed at how easily they could raise the money, not only for the food and drinks but also to put centerpieces on all the tables to make it very beautiful for everyone who attended.

I enjoyed that year at Joubert House, and I thank God every day for taking care of me throughout that part of my life.

Chapter 10
Family Court

While I was dealing with homelessness, mental health issues, and criminal trials, I was also negotiating with my wife for some kind of legal separation and divorce. Again, these hearings were held in the court in Newmarket despite my having a difficult time getting there from Toronto without a car. Because she had filed the papers in the York Region, I had to figure out how to get up there for all of these different trials. My life was extremely busy and complicated during this time, and I was happy to have a room at Joubert House to keep my legal files organized with the help of Eve Hong.

After Maria and I separated, I found myself often in Newmarket court with her, filing for a legal separation and a divorce. We were in courtroom number three in front of Justice Ronald Kaufman, a judge who had no use for me as a trans woman and made it very clear from the very first statement when he complimented Maria for "not only being a principal at a private school, but also for raising seven children," as if she was doing it on her own.

I didn't fare well in court. It was very triggering, and I was unable to get a lawyer who would actually stick with me for any length of time because I depended on legal aid, what with me being homeless. It was an uphill battle from the very beginning, which I couldn't win, but I didn't know this at the time. Access to my children was denied because of the criminal proceedings. The Parental Alienation Syndrome (PAS) argument was dismissed even though my case was a textbook definition of PAS, including getting the police involved to disparage one parent. I felt hopeless in the courtroom. I knew that the York Regional Police at 3 District were out to get me. Still, I couldn't believe that I would have such a difficult time in the justice system, which I then decided to call the legal system, because there was no sense of justice in any of their decisions. Over and over again, I would get triggered by things that were done to me, to hurt and embarrass me. I would leave deflated and depressed after having my hopes dashed once again.

I would learn in court that the land I had bought when I was twenty-one and built our dream house on was worthless. My dad had signed a letter stating that I owed Maria's father, Rocco, $460,000. I had told the judge that I would gladly acknowledge the debt if Rocco were to come into court and say it himself because I knew he couldn't lie. Maria convinced the court that he was in bad health and couldn't make the trip to Newmarket. I later read in the local newspaper that he was a medal-winning participant in the Georgina Senior Olympics. It seemed like Maria and my father had no problem lying to the courts if it served their purpose, and this worried me.

I asked the judge: if I owed Rocco $460,000, wouldn't there be some kind of paper trail of his giving me the money or my getting the money? The judge decided to ignore my father's letter unless Rocco came to court asking for the money, which he never did. Not knowing how this would get resolved triggered me into wanting to take my life. I left the courthouse, and in the forest behind the building, I broke the glass in my makeup mirror and used the glass to try to cut my wrists. When I started to bleed, it attracted ants, which crawled all over me and were biting me. So, I got up, moved thirty feet away, sat back down, and passed out. I was only out for a short time, and I woke up to find that the bleeding had stopped because my hand folded in towards me and closed the cut. I ended up going to a gas station across the road, cleaned up the blood, and took the bus back to the subway station. It was humiliating to be sitting there holding paper towels around my wrist and crying on the way back to Toronto.

At a certain point in the trial, the judge asked the York Region Children's Aid Society in Newmarket to get involved, to see if I needed to have access to my children. To my horror, the worker taking on our case was Tony Sinder, a member of our Catholic church in Georgina. I knew at that point that my chances were less than hopeless.

How could so many people hate me? What had I done that was so terrible that so many people would try so hard to separate me from my kids? These were people whom I once considered to be my friends, and they were now conspiring against me. I had a priest who said I was "possessed by the evil one." I had York Regional Police who had been at my house every day drinking coffee, sitting in my dining room or in my shop while I worked on their cars, totally ignoring my plight, and instead of trying to help a friend, they were throwing me to the wolves. I mentioned Tony Snider having his own hand in doing "God's work," keeping me from my children.

They all went out of their way to arrest me repeatedly. My very best friend, Peter Bunnik, a retired Metro Toronto police officer, would come to my house every day to drink coffee and banter with me and his police friends but did not even ask me if there was something he could do to help, even to just be a character witness for me. So many friends that I'd made through the Knights of Columbus and through the church and schools: no one would step forward and take a chance on coming to my defence. I felt persecuted like Jesus.

What could I have done to get this reaction from so many people? The answer lay not in what I had done but in who I was now perceived to be and what Maria had threatened to do if others were to speak to me. Friends of mine, Benny and Maria Bettencourt, came to Toronto to visit me in August of 2013 but were later told by my

187

ex that if they were to connect with me again, they, too, would lose access to my children. I told the Bettencourts to stay connected to my kids.

One thing you should try to keep in mind is that Maria studied child psychology as a teacher and later as a principal. She used what she learned to manipulate parents and children, and now she was using these skills to manipulate me and my children and creating a wall between us that was impenetrable. For some reason, everyone seemed to trust her, and they despised me. Even my own father and my siblings would go to court to support her and chastise me. They would glare at me in court without saying a word to me. It was heartbreaking, to say the least.

In the end, Maria spent a fortune on lawyers, taking out a mortgage on the house we had bought for my daughter to live in and extended her credit line to spend every last dime on lawyers with zero results. Not one thing was resolved in court, other than to separate me and my children for a few years. By the time Maria ran out of money, we were in mediation. She wouldn't let me talk to her in the same room, so legal aid lawyers would go between her room and my room, trying to work out a deal. Unfortunately, she was not willing to give up anything. Finally, the mediation failed as well. I found out years later that I was divorced. Somehow, the paperwork was filed and registered with the Canadian government, but I never got a copy and there was never any resolution to the separation.

I hope I'm the only one to ever have to go through this, but something tells me that this is more common than I know with transgender parents. I hope one day someone will open the files on what happened in our courtrooms and judge for themselves what's really going on in York Region. I believe the churches, the police, the lawyers, and the court officials are all homophobic and transphobic. With our newly acquired human rights, I believe that this treatment is now illegal and will have to stop.

In the end, Maria lost everything and had to move into an old house that her father owned. I wonder if she looks back on it all and thinks of it as a great waste of energy, time, and money, or does she see it as some kind of moral victory?

Our children went through hell during those years and for what? For her and me to be separated because I'm transgender? I can hardly believe that if she looks back on everything that happened, she finds it was worth it.

I love my children and to think that we lost our family because of my gender identity is too much guilt for me to bear. Our house was a peaceful sanctuary for our kids, friends, and neighbours, with no signs of marital discord. We were happy and content.

Financially, we had our problems. Maria loved to shop, and I came up with some risky ventures to try to get us more income. We ended up having too much junk, costing us a lot of money. For years, I tried in vain to get Maria to agree to stick to some kind of budget, but she thought of it as a punishment and would have nothing to do with it. Ironically, since I've been separated from her and living in a shelter, I've been able to budget and can say for certain that I haven't had any financial issues since leaving her. In fact, I often lend others money to get to the end of the month.

Christmas was very expensive for us. Not only were we spending too much on presents for family, friends, teachers, and coaches, but it was also the time that traditionally auto repairs slow down. I called these the "Visa months" because everyone seemed to be broke. January and February were always lean months and the credit card debt kept on creeping up, to the point that it was unmanageable.

I don't know when everything ended with the family courts, but eventually I just stopped having to go to mediation and everything settled down. It would be years before I found out that I was actually legally divorced.

Chapter 11
Trans History

In this chapter, I would like to chronicle the changes in my life as a transgender person over the last forty-six years to give you some idea of how far we've come, and how much it has changed my life. A lot has changed, and I think it's worth documenting this for its historical value.

When I was a child, I didn't have the words to describe who I was. At age six, in 1969, I saw some images of men dressed as women at the Stonewall Riots on our black-and-white television. I immediately knew that I identified with them but didn't appreciate to what extent it would change my life. I was never beaten for being trans. I was incarcerated, separated from my kids, and homeless, but I was never personally beaten by police.

In the early years, I didn't know there was anyone else like me and I didn't know what words to use to describe me. People used the words 'transvestite' and 'transsexual,' which I didn't relate to because I was someone who just wore dresses, and those words seemed derogatory. Also, I wasn't sure if I would ever be ready to go through with a sex change or work as a female sex worker, which seemed to be the only employment open to trans women. When I read in the back of a newspaper that there was a group in Toronto called the Canadian Cross-Dressers Club, I knew I had to go down and see who these people were. I thought *this is what describes me best*.

Talking to other cross-dressers answered a lot of my questions and the owner of the Canadian Cross Dressers Club, Paddy Aldridge, seemed to be a person who cared for our community and provided space for us to meet and mingle. Every time I went down there, I would meet new people as well as the regulars. It was interesting to see the various items of apparel that could help feminize our bodies, and see each person transform from a male image to female.

Stefonknee loves to play dress up and express her inner girl.

Holding On by a Thread

While at the club, I learned about some of the horror stories from CAMH, how they tried to use reparative therapy to get people to stop believing they are a girl. Some of the reparative techniques went so far as to use shock therapy and even frontal lobotomies to help "cure" trans women of their Gender Dysphoria. Dr. Zucker was a name that I learned to fear. I also learned that some people went to CAMH to get on a list for sex change operations, but at that time, except for that brief moment when Maria broke up with me at the Victoria Day celebrations in Mount Albert, the thought of a sex change did not seem feasible. I was now married with a family and being a father was a role that I loved and that I needed to fulfill for my children's sake.

So, for the next twenty-three years, I was content to wait for Maria to get the kids out of the house so I could quickly change into a dress and go to the city dressed as a woman or just take a bag of women's clothes with me and change down at Wildside. While dressed up, we would go out as a group to Pimblett's for dinner or hang around the club and sing karaoke. Going outside was dangerous at that time because the Toronto Police would be scouting for cross-dressers to harass or beat up if we were seen in public. Socializing with other cross-dressers was scary, but it was also enough for me to be able to express myself in public as Stephanie. At home, I wore women's lingerie to bed with my wife, which felt normal. There were a few times that I almost got caught by my kids, when they came into our room without knocking. I would have to quickly hide under the covers until Maria got them out so I could change.

After Maria asked me to leave, I had hoped that we would get back together again, so for the first six months, I just presented as female but did not consider having a sex change. What I did do was ask some of my lesbian friends to get prescriptions for birth control pills and give them to me, not knowing that the dose of estrogen was so small that it would make no difference. Unfortunately, our marriage was over and by the time I was arrested, I figured I had nothing left to lose because the restraining order meant I would no longer be able to see my children or participate in their lives.

By December 2009, with the help of my family doctor, Dr. Nasreen Ramji, I began hormone therapy. They started me on Spironolactone, a testosterone blocker, which I used for a couple months prior to starting 2.0 mg Estradiol, an estrogen supplement, and 2.5 mg Ramipril to stop blood clots caused by the Estradiol.

At this time, I was modelling for the aesthetics program at Avola College. The teacher, Joanne, knew me from before I was homeless, and when she found out that I had lost everything, she invited me to come in as a model and get my electrolysis done for free. This is when I started taking the estrogen. Joanne taught me an exercise to help my breasts grow. I would cross my arms in front of my chest and hold each elbow while flexing my pectoral muscles one hundred times in the morning and again one hundred times at night. It didn't take very long to start seeing and feeling the effects. As my breasts started to grow, they were very hard, hot, and it was very painful. But I kept doing the exercise until my breasts had grown to a D cup. Although I stopped the exercises, my breasts continued to grow to a DD cup size within a few months, which is not very common. I still go to the school every once in a while to be their model, and Joanne likes to tell all the students that she's the reason I got big breasts from the exercise she had taught me. I think she might be right.

By the time I started with the hormones, I also got a counsellor, Cecilia Schwartz. She asked me how far I wanted to go with my transition. I told her that I would like to get on the list to have a sex change, more commonly known as SRS, or Sex Reassignment Surgery. With that, she typed out a letter that we both signed that put me in contact with the CAMH Gender Identity Clinic. I was forty-six years old and hoped to have sex reassignment surgery completed within four years so that I could be done with the surgery before I turned fifty.

Later, while I was working for The 519 doing sensitivity training, we had a meeting with Dr. Anna Brown from CAMH to learn the official protocol for getting surgery. During this meeting she assured me that they did not ask those 240 questions anymore.

Those were in the past and they were too intrusive and triggering for trans women. I assured her that I had filled out that questionnaire and that it was offensive but since I needed their approval to get a sex change, I had to jump through all the hoops.

A week later, Dr. Brown called me to apologize after having seen that list in my chart. She knew that Dr. Zucker was still up to his old antics. I accepted her apology and asked if she would be my doctor at the gender clinic, which she said she would. After the phone call, she sent me a written apology. I appreciated her verifying that I was abused by the doctors, and I appreciated her caring enough to apologize.

Unfortunately, she did not last at the clinic for very long and she moved her practice to the United States six months later. I was back at the beginning, hoping to be approved for SRS. Years went by, and I was never scheduled for the surgery. Four years later, when I turned fifty in 2013, I called the clinic and told them to take me off the list. I had grown tired of waiting and I was only getting older and still suicidal.

Shortly after this, CAMH announced that Dr. Zucker would be relieved of his duties in the gender identity clinic, unfortunately with a golden handshake, which was both good news and disheartening, knowing that he would be rewarded for all the damage he had done. My life had become so complicated with the CAMH gender clinic, the courts and police, depression, and my housing situation that I couldn't see myself being in a good enough mental state to go through the physical transition anymore.

At this time, I was also advocating for Trans rights in Ontario and in the Canadian Charter of Rights. I had seen and experienced enough to know that we needed gender identity and gender expression written into our Charter of Rights because the police and hospitals were doing whatever they wanted to us.

By April 7, 2016, I had decided to have half the surgery done by paying Dr. Peter Vlaovic at Toronto East General Hospital (Michael Garron Hospital) for an orchiectomy, which was not covered by OHIP, our government medical insurance program. I had decided that this surgery would still leave the door open to get SRS if, in the future, I were to change my mind.

Over the forty-six years that I lived as a confused kid, a cross-dresser, and as a trans woman, I had seen enough and witnessed enough to know that things had to change. I was now a trans woman living in the world, isolated and stigmatized, fighting for my rights. Advocacy was beginning to shine a spotlight on our transgender community and now the average person was beginning to know that we existed.

As I write this, the urge to get SRS is still powerful and I'm approaching sixty. I feel like this is something that I still need to do for myself. I can't explain why, at fifty, it seemed impossible for me—perhaps it was the depression and constant threat of suicide.

Now, ten years later, I'm happy with my life and I feel that it is something that would complete me.

Hey Lookie Lookie!

Hey lookie lookie, see ya looking at me.

Freak in a dress, gotta set her message free.

Yeah I said HER, but for now just let it be,

Sometimes the mind…doesn't see what others see.

They put the lime in the coconut and mixed it all up,

Hey YOU! That's my coconut, oh s*** what the f***?

Made the parts in my crotch, feel freaky to me,

Something's always hang'n out, every time I go pee.

As a child I was sad, I was never happy.

No, never in a dress, it was only pants for me.

How I tried to let her out, tried to let her break free,

But they put chains on my heart, locked it up and… threw away the key.

There were rules put in place by strict society.

These things… rules and laws, never made no sense to me.

Holding On by a Thread

Even the Bible said my thoughts were blasphemy,
But again you forget, I don't see what others see.

They put the lime in the coconut and mixed it all up,
Hey YOU! That's my coconut or s*** what the f***?
May the thoughts in my head, feel funny to me.
Cuz something's got to give if you say I'm guilty.

Now Arrow slice straight, but straight ain't for me,
Somehow I'm into chicks, but you got to let it be.
In my mind I'm a babe... and to me I'm sexy.
Oh s***, what the f***? Did I just fall in love with me?

And again...
They put the lime in the coconut and mixed it all up,
Hey YOU! That's my coconut, oh s*** what the f***?
Made parts of my heart feel funny to me,
Something's always coming up, if a pretty girl I see.

So I tried to read a lot, just to clarify for me,
Why my head doesn't fit with this honk'n body,
You think it's tough being you? You ought to try being me,
It's also damn confusing, without a medical degree.

Stefonknee Wolscht

Is it nature? Is it nurture? Is it DNA ya see?

I tried to find out for myself, but they said to let it be.

They have pills to stop my tee, and give me extra pills for E.

Makes my body and my brain, that of a basket case tranny.

And all this because…

They put a lime in the coconut and mixed it all up.

Hey YOU! That's my coconut, oh s*** what the f***?

Made a t-girl from a dude, yeah exactly what you see.

Went from jeans to pretty dresses, just to set this girly free.

… and NO! You can't have my dresses, cuz they all belong to me.

Stefonknee Wolscht 2012

Chapter 12
2009–13 Pride, Trans March, Fred Victor & Kyle

I can be pretty angry and frustrated with the predicaments I get myself into, but no matter how bad things get for me, I still try to advocate for others. Through friends and allies, I'm able to do some amazing things, like help feed others who are isolated on Thanksgiving and Christmas at MCC Toronto, like march down Yonge Street with a thousand people supporting the trans community and me as I chose to lead the march through the downtown as we fought for human rights. But the proudest moment for me is always sitting in meetings and hearing the stories of other people like me who have gone through so much discrimination and hate yet are still so resilient. I'd like to think that someday, our work will make the world a better place. I can start to see it happening for younger trans children, and I hope someday it will be better for everyone, making the world a safer place to live for all.

Unfortunately, I feel like there has always been a rift between Pride Toronto and the transgender community. I don't know what happened to set us off in such different directions but somehow, Pride Toronto is all about partying and celebrating while we are advocating for the right to exist. They have a Pride parade because they think the battle is over and that things are better, but things are not yet good enough. As Pride Toronto parties their way through the month of June, dancing on the street and celebrating in bars how great life is, there are many people who are still suffering.

Both the Dyke March and the Trans March are acts of resilience against the hate that's out there towards us. Why the people at Pride Toronto choose to have a parade when there's still so much suffering going on in the world baffles me.

I have spent years sitting down with Pride Toronto to try to get them to understand why we march and why we hold vigils, including Trans Day of Visibility on March 31 and Trans Day of Remembrance (TDoR) on November 20, that caps off the end of Trans Week of Awareness, November 13-19. We need to stay united with one voice, supporting each other. We still see too much pain and suffering. There is lip service out there for many of us, but in reality, few of us benefit from the rights that we supposedly have. I understand that gay marriage and the discussions on sexuality are now mainstream, but we can't deny that people are being killed every day for being LGBTQ2+ throughout the world. We need to rally and support our brothers and sisters who are out there suffering and being persecuted. Pride Toronto has massive resources to pull off spectacular shows and parties, yet they do very little to help the community. When asked for a budget to help pay for marginalized trans performers, year after year, out of the $5,000,000 annual budget that they have, we were given nothing. In 2014, they agreed to provide me with $200 for each performer on the trans stage in the previous year, so all in all, it cost them $800. Eight hundred dollars out of $5 million is a sad reflection of what Pride stands for. It's not that we are lacking the talent, but we are lacking the resources we need to survive. I hope and pray that one day, this event that we hold through Pride Toronto in June every year will spend more money on lifting people out of poverty and out of their precarious lives into a world that we could all be proud of. I hope we give a voice to all the people who suffer in silence.

Despite the lack of funds, every year since 2009, the Trans March has been held—initially against the will of Pride Toronto—on the Friday of Pride weekend, the last weekend in June to coincide with the Stonewall Riots of 1969. The trans community and their friends, families, and allies march in Toronto, and this year marks another year of standing proud and resilient against the hate and discrimination that is out there. The trans community has a lot to celebrate: we have human rights protection throughout Canada. But we don't march because we choose to celebrate, but rather because our march is about all those who are still suffering and to shine a spotlight on the problems throughout the world.

When I march, I carry the Ugandan flag because it is illegal to be transgender in Uganda, it is illegal to be gay or lesbian in Uganda, and it is impossible for someone from Uganda to march with a Ugandan flag, even in Toronto. So, I hold their flag for them, and we stand in solidarity with them and their struggles. One day this world will be a better place for all LGBTQS2+ people, and then I'll be ready to raise a glass and toast how great we are as humans, showing kindness towards each other. Until then, I'll put my celebration on the back burner and help our neighbours throughout the world.

At the opening ceremony for World Pride in 2014, on a stage in front of Toronto City Hall, I remember when Pride Toronto's then-executive director, Kevin Beaulieu, announced to the world that it was time to listen to the trans community and not speak for them. Everyone told me that I should meet with him and talk to him again about importance of changing the "Trans Parade" to a "Trans March" that would include a wreath-laying ceremony for trans people who have been killed.

Kickoff of World Pride Toronto at Nathan Phillips Square (June 20, 2014)

It felt like Kevin was beginning to understand. I met with him the following Monday and we discussed listening to the trans community. He responded that it was too late for that year because everything was already in place.

So, what happened? We showed the world that the trans community in Toronto would be having a trans parade rather than a memorial march. The actual truth is that we would not have needed to get a parade permit, we could just march in defiance of those that oppress us. I didn't attend the trans march that year. That was the year that we filmed *Paul Wears Dresses*. In fact, I haven't participated in the Trans March since then. I feel strong again this year, and, I will march again, not because life is so great but to show others there is hope.

Prior to COVID-19, there was an agency in Toronto that catered to the transgender community, the Fred Victor employment centre. The centre would open early on Mondays just for the trans community to come in and get counseling or look for job placements and socialize with trans people who quite often had no place else to go. William Hines, a counselor and trans activist, went out of his way to make everyone feel welcome. When Kyle Scanlon passed away, it was William, heartbroken at losing such an active ally and great friend, who spearheaded Kyle's memorial. His family refused to accept him as a man, even in death. I totally understand why we need to get special treatment when we are so marginalized and isolated, living in fear of when the next attack or arrest will happen. It's through agencies like the Fred Victor that we are able to get a leg up, to find work that helps us survive.

I have an amazing story to share with you about an agency that I've started to use in Parkdale, where I now live. The Parkdale Queen West Community Health Centre is where I found health professionals who serve our marginalized community. I started going to the Centre worried that I might not fit in, that maybe I'd be in a group of older people like me, who might not understand or might not be supportive. I was wrong. I have found a supportive place that treats me like your average cisgender woman. At the Coping with Diabetes group, the chiropodist, the Women of Wonder group, or the physiotherapist and counseling, I am treated and respected for the woman I am. It doesn't have to be about my being transgender: I interact with other clients, and they respect my name and my pronouns and treat me as an equal. We learn, laugh, and have fun. I need to acknowledge that the work that Jane, Christine, Debra, Anna-Marie, Kurti, and Jenny do with us as a group, which gives me a place to go to feel safe, normal, and beautiful, is exactly what I need to be safe. It is at times like this that I believe things are getting better, and I truly believe that one agency at a time, transgender lives will flourish. It's a small step, but it is a step forward and I am truly grateful for that.

My church, MCC Toronto, is a safe place that welcomes all who enter for worship, fellowship, or because they need help. They have seen me crying uncontrollably and comforted me. They provide a venue for the trans community to meet and discuss events to draw attention to our situation. They march with us at Pride, and they make it known to the world that transgender rights are important across the globe. They stand with us in solidarity and hold us up when we feel defeated.

I cannot say enough about all those kind people who have been there for me when I couldn't go on and tried to end my life. The doctors, nurses, social workers, counsellors, friends, and neighbours who kept me alive in my darkest moments, all have my gratitude for everything they've done. I would be remiss to not mention some friends - Laura, Lisa and Imelda, that are now supporting me and have turned me on to supporting the Blue Jays here in Toronto. Laura was my fresh set of eyes to check the final text of this book.

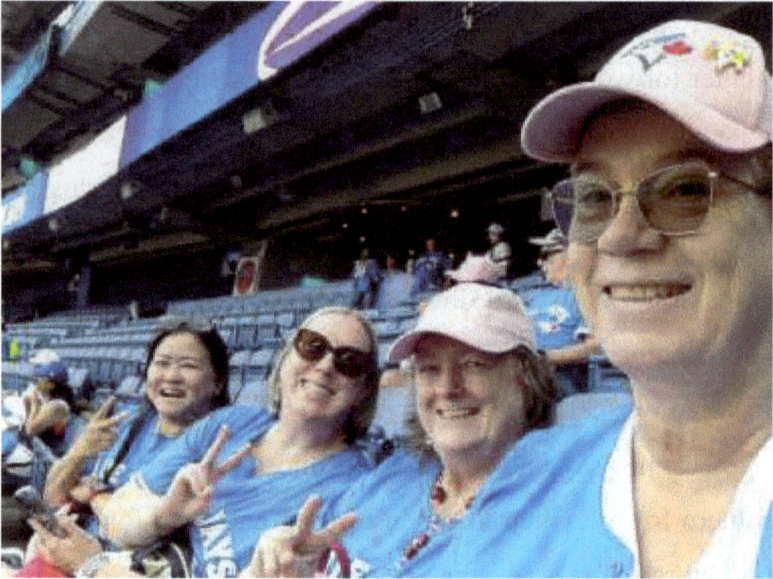

Imelda Lim, Lisa & Laura Bennett & Steffy

Where is Pride?

In an article in the *Toronto Star* dated July 4, 2010, a reporter writes about Brian Burke, the general manager of the Toronto Maple Leafs at that time, who marched in the Pride parade in Toronto for his son, Brendan Burke, who was gay and had passed away. The article showed a high-profile father proud of his gay son; unfortunately, his son was not alive to see his dad march for him.

I wonder if this article would ring true for me?

I know many friends who have their families' support, but to go out and stand side by side and march with them or for them is a much bigger testament to their love.

Unfortunately, I have never felt that kind of love from my father or my wife. I see them in court every time I am expected to appear, but they never have a kind word to say. They use the opportunity to embarrass, ridicule, and humiliate me. When they look at me and see a trans woman, their body language and words express their disgust and rage.

Love? I often wonder if they could ever love someone like me way down inside. Even my wife of twenty-three years, the woman who married me, has destroyed my life after asking me to leave because I could not suppress these feelings and "start acting like a man." She and my father have done everything they could to leave me mentally depressed, homeless, and isolated. She could not understand the negative effects these words and attitudes would have on someone like me.

The stigma attached to mental illness, the stigma attached to being homeless, and the stigma attached to identifying as transgendered multiply the hatred towards me, to a point where anyone who hears the story of what has happened feels the need to comfort her. She felt justified in pressing criminal charges against me three months after I left my home quietly, in order to keep something like me away from her and our children. The police and the justice system felt justified in prosecuting me to protect my wife and children.

The legal system seems to feel that by restraining my activity and my rights, they are somehow making my children's lives safer and better. They look at me like a self-serving, selfish individual, set on making these trials all about herself. When suggesting that this is not just about me and expecting me to seek more treatment and counselling for myself, they would not extend that help to my children. I have found many good counsellors over the years, but my wife and the courts refuse to acknowledge these services or endorse and extend these services to my children. They say that I am making this all about me? They, by their very actions of arresting, charging, and convicting me of criminal wrongdoing, crimes that would not be considered an assault if I were to identify as a "normal" man, are endorsing that very idea and confirming the fact that this is all about me.

I often dream of finding some form of peace. I wonder why God has led us down this path. I hope and pray that someday I will not be so alone.

I can't help but wonder… unlike Brendan Burke, will anyone stand up and march with or for me now?

Or only after I am gone?

(((((((((((Hugs)))))))))))) Stefonknee Wolscht

Chapter 13
109 Pembroke Street

Days turned into weeks and weeks turned into months, and in that time, I went from the shelter to transitional housing. After a year at Joubert House, I was offered an apartment in supportive housing at 109 Pembroke St., on my own with a key to lock my door and an apartment where I would feel safe.

I got the apartment because it had been empty for three months and condemned; it was uninhabitable. The ceiling was falling down, and the floors were disgusting; the previous tenant had not cleaned up after their cats, so the flooring needed to be torn out and the ceiling needed to be replaced. The whole apartment needed a thorough cleaning.

It took me three months to fix up apartment five at 109 Pembroke Street. When it was done, I had my own kitchen, living room, big bedroom, and a private bathroom with tub and shower, the first time in two years that I was able to take a bath. This was still affiliated with Street Haven and was known as supportive housing. I still had social workers, Anne and Krista, who would help me with any complicated forms or trials and tribulations my life was full of. The difference was that I got to choose when and if we met.

I moved into my new apartment at the end of January 2011, once I'd got the place ready and livable. I quickly started inviting people to come and visit and hang out in my apartment. It was nice to be able to invite people in. At the shelter we were not allowed to have guests, and even in transitional housing, we still had to ask our housemates' permission before we could invite anybody into the house, so it was challenging to entertain.

When I unlocked my door at 109 Pembroke Street, I would fully expect to see myself dead inside my apartment. I felt like a ghost. I'm a ghost because I have lost so many people in my life—friends and relatives—that I often wondered if I had just passed away and no one told me that I was gone. My family had totally erased me because I'm transgender. So, when my father died on January 1, 2013, and no one told me that he was dying or that he had passed away, it reinforced these feelings that I was no longer among the living. On January 13, his ghost came and visited me. He would visit me for the next three nights but stopped visiting me once I told him that I forgave him for what he had done. It's a very weird feeling to know that nobody wants you in their life.

Unfortunately, being in the apartment was not safe for me. Looking to find myself dead in there, either in the bathroom, in the bed, or on the couch in the living room, was very surreal and very confusing, but having attempted suicide so many times, it was part of my reality. My mind was also clouded from the Seroquel, so I would often think that I was a ghost.

To help me cope with my depression and feeling unsafe in my apartment, the shelter staff allowed me to come down and sit in the dining room if I felt unsafe at home. So, on many occasions I found myself ringing the doorbell and talking to the staff and either sitting in the dining room or doing dishes in the kitchen all night to keep myself distracted from my thoughts. If the staff on duty felt I was in no condition to be on my own, they would call for an assessment team from the Gerstein Crisis Center to assess my mental state and decide whether I needed to be admitted into the hospital again. This went on for years.

It was about this time, in the summer of 2011, that I was leaving Sherbourne Health Center, about to cross the street, when a stranger started screaming at me. The next thing I knew, he was picking up stones from the garden of one of the buildings and throwing them at me as I was crossing the street with all the cars. I was infuriated and went back, running towards him to defend myself. With one punch, I knocked him down on the ground, and I started walking away again. He didn't get up and never did connect with any of the stones that he was throwing, but I was so angry that people could be so transphobic. Incidents like this made me feel the need to advocate for strict laws against trans hate crimes and discrimination.

At 109 Pembroke, things were different. I could leave my door unlocked and allow neighbours and friends to come in and make themselves at home whenever they wanted to. It was really nice having the company, and I'm sure my neighbours enjoyed having a place to go for a coffee to get a break from the isolation of living independently again. After a while, Lorraine, Don, and I set up the backyard with a patio set. Everyone in our building would enjoy our shaded backyard, whether sitting out there to enjoy the fresh air or just relaxing on the porch swing. We had a lot of fond memories of being out there.

There were other women in the building whom I knew from my days at Street Haven. We all got along great and would spend hours socializing in the backyard. Moving out of the shelter was a milestone for each of us as we became more independent.

I hit an all-time low on August 23, 2013, the day before my daughter Amanda was to be married to her fiancé, Dave Sita. I had met with our family friends Benny and Maria Bettencourt a few months earlier and they had shown me an invitation they received to Amanda's wedding on the 24th. They were taken aback when they heard that I was not invited to go to the wedding. They promised me that they would talk to Amanda and see if she would reconsider.

Shortly after that, I received a message from Amanda stating that I could "come to the wedding itself if I dressed as a man, sat at the back, and agreed not to talk to anyone." I could not understand how she expected me to be in a church full of friends, family, and my children and not be able to talk to anyone while being dressed as a man at the back of the service. I was heartbroken, and as it drew closer to her wedding day, I was losing control. Not only was my dad not going to be there because of his passing earlier that year, but also her own father wouldn't be walking her down the aisle, supporting her and her new life.

I ended up going to the Gerstein Crisis Center so I could be safe on Amanda's wedding day. As I was painting a picture as a wedding gift for her, everything fell apart. Another client there went into my room, which did not have a lock, and went through my stuff. They took all of my valuables, including all my money, which was just over $300. I saw lottery tickets in all the garbage cans and didn't realize he was buying them with my money. But when I went back up to my room before supper, I found all my stuff strewn around and my valuables were gone. The staff said they couldn't do anything because they couldn't prove that he had done it, so I took this as a sign from God to go and just kill myself. I was walking home and as I passed through Allan Gardens, two young men started to harass me. I was furious, so I grabbed the one man's headphones off of his head, broke them and chased them out of the park. When I got home to my apartment, I attempted suicide once more.

Because I had left Gerstein in tears, they had called the police to go and check in on me. I don't remember the police coming, but when I woke up, I was back at St. Michael's Hospital in the emergency recovery area. They ended up admitting me to the 17th floor again for another psych evaluation.

I only stayed in the hospital for a few days because the doctors felt that I was safe to go home after I explained the situation about the wedding.

When my father died on Jan 1, 2013, and after his ghost had visited me, I struggled with memories of what I could have done wrong. I was unaware that he had been sick or that he had passed on. If not for his ghost coming to my apartment, I would have been oblivious to his passing. I would spend the next few days reminiscing about my childhood and wondering what I could have done differently to get my dad to like me.

I remember when I was a little child, going to the bakery in Toronto with my dad and older sister, Monica, on Saturday mornings. We spent countless hours in the bakery having fun, packing buns into bags while learning to count to twelve. I remember flour dust on the machines, the smell of fresh baking in the air, and so many friendly faces that made our time there special. I liked going to the bakery and getting to know everyone who worked there.

I also remember one day on the farm because of an old photo. We were sitting in the bucket of our front loader with our cousins, up in the air, looking over the edge of the bucket to get a picture taken. It was a hot summer day, and we were all in our bathing suits about to go out to Lake Simcoe to go swimming. We were in front of the barn and my cousins made a fuss about the smell of the cows, which made us laugh—they were real city kids.

I also remember my dad teaching us to swim up at the lake. He'd throw a dollar into the water at the end of the dock and watch us jump in to see whoever could get it first, because we got to keep it. Thank God it was still paper money back then and the dollar floated on top of the water. Those were the good times, and there were lots of good memories.

Tragedy struck our farm on March 8, 1980, at two-thirty in the morning. We woke to a bright light flickering in our bedrooms: the barn was on fire. My dad and I raced out the door in our pajamas. We ran into the bottom of the barn to start opening up doors to let the animals out while the fire was raging above our heads. Upon entering the barn, I tripped on something hidden by the thick smoke and fell in the manure, covering my face in cow feces. We managed to open up all the doors to let the animals out before having to retreat from the smoke and run outside for fresh air. Unfortunately, most of the animals did not come out of the dark until the fire department got there and started spraying water from their hoses into the open doors to clear the smoke. Suddenly about forty pigs came running out with their backs on fire but alive. The fireman doused the flames on each pig, as they went on to sleep in the corn pit, munching away happily. They were safe. When I saw my dad's face, it was red and blistered from the heat; my having fallen in the manure cooled off my face and protected me from the hot flames.

Unfortunately, two mother sows, their piglets and two calves never made it out of the burning barn. I had nightmares for years thinking about how horrible it must have been for them. The charred remains of the barn continued smoldering for the next five days.

We would eventually put a roof over the foundation of the barn, but we would never see it back in its true glory with its hip roof and hayloft.

Later that day I sketched a picture of the barn and included the article in the newspaper and the details of the deaths, which I still have today. We believe the barn was intentionally burned down to force us to sell our land to subdivision developers. It didn't work; we kept farming for a couple more decades.

Sketch of our farmyard prior to fire. March 8, 1980, by Stefonknee Wolscht

There was a lot of work on the farm, but it made us strong and unique because we learned the value of work at a very young age. We were rewarded by having our own calves or pigs to invest our money in. For all his faults, my dad taught me two important things: how to invest money and how to drink beer. I know what you're thinking and it's not that. My dad taught me that if he went to the fridge for a beer, he could take a couple of sips, put a rubber cap on top of the bottle, and save the rest for another time. Just because the beer was open didn't mean it all had to be drunk. All of my siblings to this day are really good with money and none of us have a drinking problem, so thanks, Dad.

My mom was a typical farm wife. She was in the kitchen early in the morning and in the fields throughout the day, and then back in the kitchen late at night. She worked so hard and tirelessly to provide for us and keep us safe. She was my dad's right-hand helper, always learning and always taking the lead when my father was gone to work. Some would say we took on too much and it was a little chaotic at times, but to this day, I still love taking the lead from my mom and pitching in no matter what or no matter how chaotic something may seem to be. I love you, Mom. Rest in peace.

Having four siblings on the farm meant that there was a lot of laughter and a lot of fighting. I remember my brothers Michael and Eric would often wrestle and tease each other about who could do things faster; they were very competitive. Since Michael was older, he often would defeat Eric in the fight, so I would often get them mad at me so that the two of them could take me on, which seemed like a fair fight since I was two years older. These little battles would go on until one day, Eric grew taller than his brother and he stopped Michael in his tracks. Michael would never challenge Eric again from that day forward. They are still best friends to this day.

My sister spent a lot of time babysitting my youngest brother, Robert, in the house while we were out in the fields. Robert was eight years younger than me, so to me, he was always the little one. I'm old enough to remember the introduction of computers and I remember my little brother getting his first Commodore 64 and us playing tennis with a bouncing light on the screen.

We were a good family. We went to church every Sunday and we were active members in our church. I was an altar server, and my dad was an usher. I can still remember the smell of incense that permeated the walls of that building and the bright light that shone through the yellow stained-glass windows. We didn't live in the same town as Our Lady of Good Counsel church, but people knew we were there, and they respected us and welcomed us into their community. Overall life was pretty good—except for what we never talked about that happened in private at home.

Holding On by a Thread

I lived at 109 Pembroke until the evening of May 11, 2016. That afternoon, while I was away, a drug dealer on the top floor set fire to his apartment, which set off the sprinkler system throughout the building. It was a complete loss, and everyone who lived there was homeless once again. Most of our belongings were destroyed by the smoke and water damage. It was heartbreaking. I went from having everything in my previous life to leaving the hospital with two bags of clothes, a phone, and my computer seven years earlier, only to lose everything once again.

Why did everything have to be so hard? I didn't have any insurance to protect my belongings; I didn't think that something like this could happen to me.

By October 1, I had given up waiting for them to fix our apartments because I had to live in my car when I wasn't staying with friends in Peterborough. So, in October of 2016, I moved into my present-day apartment in Parkdale and got a cat, Mykoto-kun, to keep me company because I was no longer with all my friends from Street Haven. I continue to live in Parkdale and have made many new friends. I finally transitioned to living on my own without any external support, managing to start a new life.

Chapter 14
G8/G20 Toronto

During the time that I was living at Joubert House, in the summer of 2010, I was a part of the G8/G20 Summit protests in Toronto. I felt that the summit was for the rich and powerful, and now, being in the shelter system made me hate that world. I remember summits prior to this one, such as the summit in Montreal in October of 2000. There, protesters used the media spotlight to highlight government corruption and wrongdoing, so I felt this would be worth my while, joining rallies and becoming an activist. The world leaders of the G8 and G20 nations would have to hear our message on the news, even though their meetings were behind closed doors.

On June 22, a warm Friday afternoon, we held a Gender Justice March and I found myself at the front of the protest, holding a gender justice banner and leading the march. The police were there in full force. Most of them were on bikes and they used their bikes to line the road and keep us guided in one direction; they'd brought in police from all over Canada. The federal government had given them a budget of 1 billion dollars to cover security for the week-long event. I remember laughing when I saw the number of cameras that they had on top of vehicles to take our pictures. I was at the front protesting, and I'm sure they got a million photos of me. Not only did they have surveillance equipment and bicycle cops, but there were also snipers posted on top of buildings throughout the city. The downtown core was cordoned off with roadblocks and fences, and it seemed like the citizens of Toronto had moved out for the week and left behind a ghost town.

We started off at Carlton Street, right near Allan Gardens, marched west, and didn't stop till we got to Yonge Street. The police saw a homeless guy sitting along the way on the sidewalk minding his own business, so they stopped our march to harass him, eventually arresting him. They picked him up and took him away; this foreshadowed what was going to happen later on that week. We continued across College, then turned south on University Avenue and stopped at Elm Street. It was there that they decided to end the protest with a wall of police officers kneeling down with a row of shields, then a line of police with guns, and then behind them were police mounted on horses—all in riot gear. At this point, all the bicycle police left the scene, and I was in a standoff, alone with these police in the middle of the street.

Stefonknee Wolscht

A TV image of Stefonknee standing up to the police barricade at the G8/20 June 22, 2010

Being at the front of the march, I had no idea what was happening behind me. Everyone had stopped about a hundred metres away from this group of police officers that blocked the entire road. I had walked up to the front of the barricade when I looked over my shoulder and saw everyone had stayed back about a hundred yards and a bunch of media were moving in the opposite direction. They noticed me single-handedly taking on these cops, and that's when a bunch of the journalists came running up, just as I put my head over the shield of one officer and asked him if that's where we were going to dance. At that point, an officer to my right yelled at me to step back, so I took one giant step backwards, at which he repeated, "I told you to step back."

I responded with, "I stepped back, now you step back," which was a bit of a joke because with them clad in their riot gear and the horses behind them, they would have fallen over like dominos had they tried. It got a good laugh from all the police officers, and everything remained calm, but I'll never forget plugging up the street when they made us turn around and go back towards Queen's Park.

Imagine a middle-aged Catholic father of seven and a pillar in my church just two years earlier, now standing up to the police and demanding human rights. I felt like my community had deceived me and that I was sold a bill of goods, that if I didn't conform to their definition of 'normal,' then they would persecute me, which they had. The police were no longer my friends as they had been for over twenty years; now, they were pointing guns and screaming at me. Common courtesies that I had taken for granted for so many years were nowhere to be found. It was now us or them, and they held all the power.

The protest ended quietly that day, and we had sent our message to the media that trans rights are human rights and that we needed to advance human rights protection throughout Canada.

On June 23, I went up to Barrie on the route that the leaders were taking into Muskoka to stand on a bridge over Highway 400 with a protest sign as the G8 attendees went up to Huntsville, hoping to send them a message that we wanted human rights. On the way up, I noticed that my phone was jammed, and my GPS wouldn't work anywhere near the convoy. The police had spent a lot of money on equipment such as signal jammers, sound cannons, and video recording equipment to use on the protesters.

When we marched down Queen Street the next day, we saw a police car sitting in the middle of the road with no one in it. It was a beat-up old cruiser, abandoned in the middle of the street with no police in sight. We all marched past it but soon someone jumped on the roof and started smashing the windows. We could tell by the yellow oval symbol on the bottom of their boot that they were undercover police officers, and they were making us look like hoodlums, vandalizing public property. The same group would later set the car on fire and went around smashing windows in downtown Toronto businesses. We paid no mind to them, and we told others to ignore what they were doing and just continue to march and stay focused on our messages.

The day after, the media made it sound as though the protesters had started the fire and were out of control. As a group, we knew that these were agent provocateurs who were going out of their way to make us look bad, which made us work harder to keep everyone peaceful. The media would later report that the boots of those protesters damaging public property were the boots of police officers. Rather than keeping the peace, the police were a public nuisance and made common citizens who were trying to send a message to the world look like hooligans.

Another day, I was part of the bike rally, but the protesters got caught out in a rainstorm that hindered all activity. Little did I know that while we were protesting in the downtown core, there was a group of protesters just to the west of us at Queen and Spadina who were surrounded by police and kept outside, wet and cold, to suffer in the rain. I think that had I known what the police were doing to this group, I might have broken the law that day to come to their defence. It wasn't until I saw the news that evening that I realized the police had singled out that group to 'kettle' and arrest.

The police were constantly kettling or corralling protesters, which meant surrounding them and arresting them to take them to a detention center on Eastern Avenue. The most notable person beaten and arrested was Adam Nobody, a twenty-seven-year-old man whom police assaulted and took into custody and later put on trial. His beating was videotaped, and that tape was later used in court to prove that he was innocent. Despite the video, the police chief, Bill Blair, insisted that Adam had attacked the police officers. The officer who kicked Adam in the face was never charged.

Like the police who told me to step back on day one, it seemed that the cops who wanted to cause the most trouble came from Calgary and were there for a fight. None of us took the bait, but they did manage to arrest and beat up a lot of innocent people just for being there and taking part in the protest. Of all the people taken to the holding cells on Eastern Avenue, and of the fewer who were actually charged, not a single person was convicted. Like the homeless man sitting on the sidewalk the first day, many were victims of just being in the wrong place at the wrong time.

I am sure the exposure we got helped promote trans rights, as well as stimulate the Truth and Reconciliation meetings for Indigenous people, so some good did come from it all. With my friends in Toronto and Ottawa, we were able to move mountains with our hard work to secure a better Canada for all transgender people.

Today, children learn about gender diversity in kindergarten and throughout elementary school, and young adults learn about gender identity and gender expression in high schools, colleges, and universities.

Workplace sensitivity training is promoted across Canada. Trans people can now step forward safely, knowing that they cannot be discriminated against. This was the main reason for me to write my autobiography because all these changes took place in my lifetime. In fact, from the moment I started transitioning in 2009 until 2017, Canada became a safer place for transgender people, and what happened to me will never have to happen to anyone again in housing, the legal system or any institutions that provide services for gender diverse individuals. I'm really proud that I was able to join in this effort with many of my friends.

Chapter 15
Occupy Toronto

On October 15, 2011, a group of about 3,000 protesters converged in Toronto's financial district at a rally that would soon become Occupy Toronto.

We gathered at the corner of King and Bay Streets and soon marched east across King Street to St. James Park. Occupy was a grassroots organization that tried to take power from the 1%, mainly the banks, and spread it equally among the 99%, the ordinary people who were struggling in the world.

Although we agreed that there would be no leaders in Occupy Toronto, I soon realized that Sakura Saunders, Dave Vasey, Lana Brite, Katie Berger, and Taylor Chelsea were passionate about saving our planet and saving the 99%. I thought they would be able to inspire everyone to take up the cause. To this day, with the exception of Dave Vasey, who passed away—rest in peace, dear friend—these young people are still working to make the world a better place. These people were, in my opinion, natural leaders when it came to keeping everyone organized and keeping us focused on the tasks at hand.

I showed up early to the rally with my truck and my sound system, ready to help in any way I could. Unfortunately, they said they wouldn't use it because they would use "the people's mic." That meant everyone repeating what someone at the front of the group said and it would echo down through the group outward to the buildings like the telephone game, just much louder. So, once we started to move out of the downtown financial district, I followed at the back of the march and only used my sound system once we got to St. James Park. Once we arrived at the park, we immediately set up tents, and we made it very clear that we would occupy the area in the park for the foreseeable future.

Just like every Occupy movement around the world, ours was a spin-off of the uprising that was happening in the Arab Spring and Occupy Wall Street. Occupy Toronto was continuously surrounded by journalists of every kind, and they kept asking us the same question: "What were we hoping to accomplish?"

We answered the same way every time. "We hope to get rid of the control that big multinational corporations and banks have over the common people and to take the power away from the 1% and spread it among the rest of society, the 99%." That meant listening to all marginalized groups that were at Occupy, common workers, and the middle class to hear what they needed in order to get equality. For me, it was trans rights. We had the media's attention and used it along with all the groups around the world to shine a light on what was going wrong with capitalism.

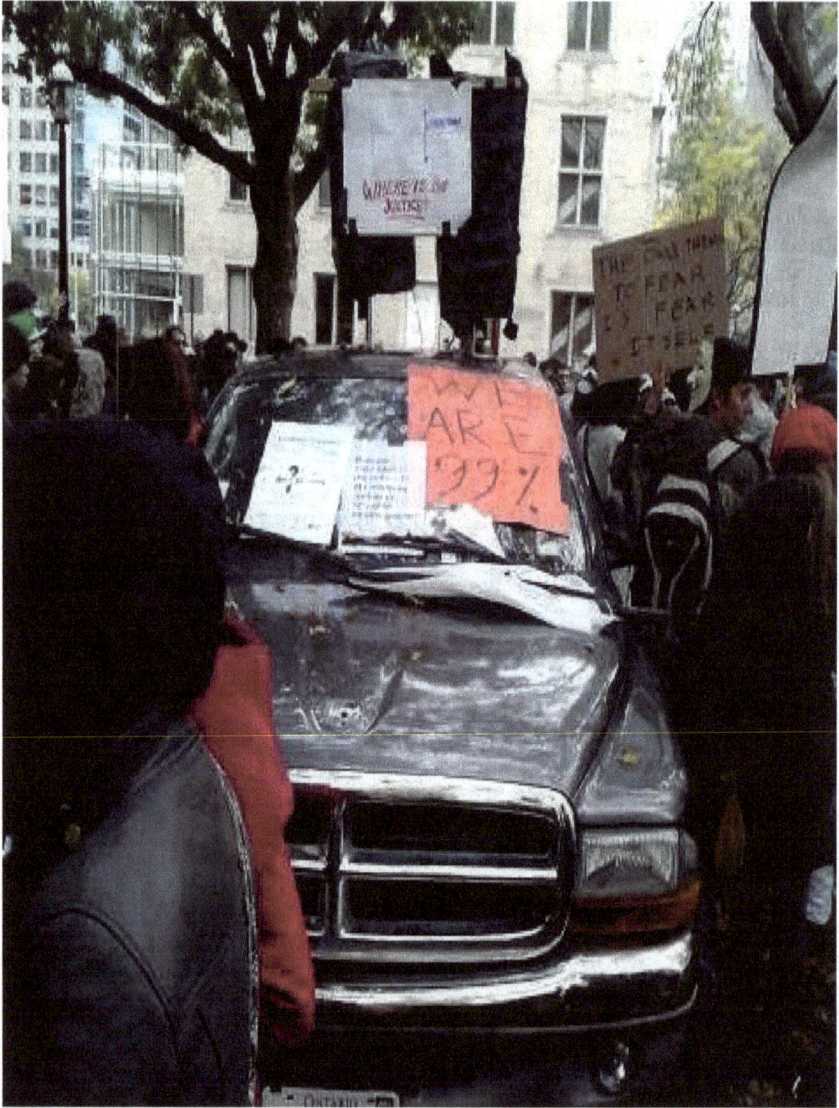

Stefonknee and her truck at Occupy Toronto (October 15, 2011)

One morning, in our first week there, we woke up after a massive storm and found a lot of trees uprooted and branches scattered throughout the park. An elderly Indigenous man walked with me through the park, assessing the damage and said something which I'll never forget. He said, "Who will teach the young trees when all the old trees are gone?"

As a Catholic, this was very profound and made me wonder why my church did not protect the trees and include Mother Nature in our spirituality.

I made a lot of friends there and I helped manage logistics for the occupation in Toronto. Part of my job was to create an electrical system in the park for the media tent, meeting spaces, medical tent, and library. Someone donated two beautiful yurts, one for a library and the other for holding smaller meeting groups, which was also a women's safe space. These yurts kept us warm and dry on cold, wet days. There was also a gazebo in the centre of the park where we held the larger outdoor meetings for everyone at Occupy. With the trees that were damaged from the storm, we started a sacred fire and somehow kept it going throughout the month despite the wood being green and wet. Splitting firewood was a great pastime for a lot of the younger occupiers who enjoyed doing physical labour to let some steam out.

The entire time that we were in the park, we were constantly being interviewed by every kind of media and were often the lead story of the day and front-page news. We did hundreds of interviews and dominated the news at that time, which got us really good exposure. While we were occupying the park, the police guarded the perimeter and sent agent provocateurs into our midst to make getting consensus nearly impossible at meetings. Every day, we would march to various spots in the city to highlight different marginalized people.

I remember one march in particular, the Indigenous march, where, for the first time, we were told we could not walk on the road but instead had to march on the sidewalks and respect traffic lights. This infuriated me. I took my truck with the sound system in the back, put a microphone into the front, and got one of the Indigenous drummers to drum as loud as he could while my amp was turned up as high as possible. We parked in every intersection, blocking traffic as the other marchers waited for the light to change colour. I totally lost it. I took my truck alone up Bay Street to the financial district and then up to Queen and Bay by City Hall and refused to leave despite people coming down from the towers complaining about the noise. Eventually, our group caught up to us and we took over the entire intersection. Later we would move to Dundas and Yonge and shut down Canada's busiest intersection with Indigenous dancing and speeches.

I loved being at Occupy Toronto because there were a lot of young, enthusiastic people there who wanted to make the world a better place. I loved listening to what they had to say and how they hoped to make the 1% pay for their greed. Being in the midst of these young people felt like I was home with my kids again; many of the people at St. James Park were the same age as my children.

One such person, going by the name of Jeffrey, turned out to be a younger version of myself, just seventeen years old and living alone in Toronto. They started coming to the rallies presenting as female, with pink hair and beautiful makeup on. Jeffrey and I would quickly become friends. They were very technically savvy and would help with media relations in the media tent, while I was setting up the infrastructure in logistics. Our friendship has lasted to this day. Jeffrey is now thirty years old, and they just finished writing their first book, *Sun Circle, a Magical Solar Grimoire* by J.R. Damon, and have since bought their first house.

Jeffrey and Stefonknee being our fabulous selves

Jeffrey and I got up to all sorts of silly stuff like dressing up and visiting the St. Lawrence market looking like Christmas elves and making it onto the CBC news, to get their audience to feel more festive. Jeffrey was also into witchcraft, and one time, we went to Lady Tamara's house, where she mentored them, and I offered myself as a human sacrifice if they needed one. Needless to say, I'm still here but we had a good laugh over the whole ordeal. It was nice to know Jeffrey during this time and watch them grow as I should have watched my kids mature.

When I was at Occupy Toronto, I was the only person wearing a dress at first who was male, or transgender. I worried that in that environment, I could get assaulted because there were people who hated us for being activists and they were coming into the park looking to start fights. Ironically, within a few days, more transgender people who were part of our community started to wear dresses to occupy the park as well. One day, while I was at the logistics tent working, a fight broke out in front of my tent. I went out to see two men arguing and one of the men took his shoe and stomped on the other man's foot; he was wearing sandals, so I could see the blood start to pool on the ground. Here I was in my dress, and I lost it. I picked the guy up, dropped him to the ground, and started pummeling his face. I was tired of people coming into the park and trying to hurt us, and I took it out on this poor guy. When it was done, I ended up with a gash on my right hand from his cheekbone and his face was all bloodied. Afterwards he went to the police, who arrived a few minutes later while I was bandaging my right hand. A police officer asked what had happened and I explained it, and I showed them the other guy's foot bandaged. They asked if either of us wanted to press charges against this poor guy standing there with blood all over his face. I asked that he just be banned from entering the park and that he not be charged. As they left, they warned him not to come back into the park and I chuckled, thinking *he's got a bloody face and I've got a bloody fist but because he attacked with the first strike, he's the one being punished for starting a fight.*

Another time at St. James Park, an undercover police officer was harassing a group of spectators at the gazebo, trying to pick a fight. I approached him and told him to cool down or leave the area. He immediately pushed me down the hill and started attacking other people. I got up, grabbed him by the collar of his shirt, and pushed him down into a hedge, pushing his head down against the branches, which cut the back of his head and his blond hair quickly started turning red. The crowd then turned on him and ended up chasing him out of the park. Some police came to his rescue, taking him aside but not dealing with the angry mob. This is why we figured he must have been an undercover police officer, an agent provocateur.

I wasn't always a violent person, but the people who attacked me, or my friends, would soon find out that I would not back away but would defend myself. Sometimes, we need to stand up to bullies and put them in their place. I've never been arrested for defending myself or standing up for others.

Chapter 16
MCCT & Mental Health: Linda Leenders and Allison Hannaford

Living with trauma made me very self-aware of my every reaction. Always wondering if I was being judged for my weaknesses and vulnerabilities, I was extremely cognizant that I tried too hard to please people and worked too hard to make friends. I wanted everyone to like me, and I had a problem with boundaries. My doctors finally diagnosed me with depression, anxiety, complex PTSD, and borderline personality disorder. They warned me about making sure I had boundaries and limits to what I was willing to do to please people. The borderline personality disorder is what made me misread cues and wait for people to show their approval before continuing to try to make them my friends. This also caused me to question my presence in social interactions. I'm always wondering why people are interested in me or why they like me.

As a child, I didn't know that I had a mental disorder, and in those days, it wouldn't have been talked about anyway, even if I had known. It was considered a weakness, and we did not show weakness as boys and young men or see a psychologist or a psychiatrist; therapy was frowned upon. The physical abuse seemed normal; it was just a part of getting disciplined. It wouldn't be until

I had a complete breakdown in 2009 that my doctors started to investigate my issues and provide therapy so I could move forward and be healed.

I met a lot of really lovely people in the hospitals. Patients could be your neighbour, your friend, or even a member of your family, people who had developed a hard outer shell to protect themselves from vulnerabilities and the outside world, with all its judgment, just to stay safe.

From July 2009 until September 2020, I spent a lot of time crying, keeping to myself, and surviving despite all the obstacles and hurdles put in my way. I know for a fact that some of my therapists were saddened by what was happening to me because, at times, they would wipe away tears of their own. When this happened, I felt like I was hurting them by sharing what had happened and I felt like I needed to protect them from my pain, so I would shut down and hold back. That would make my trauma even harder to deal with because I was afraid to say what had really happened for fear that I would hurt those who were caring for me.

I remember nurses and doctors sitting in my room and just casually chatting with me about good things, small talk, things that would make us laugh. It was nice to laugh, even if it was through tears; it showed they cared, and it made me feel human. When they empathized with me, I would easily befriend them and confide in them with some of the things that I wouldn't tell other doctors and nurses.

A friend and a counsellor for me was my church deacon, Linda Leenders. She went above and beyond when it came to trying to understand me. I met her at MCC Toronto in the spring of 2010. She was a deacon at the church, but she also ran a support group called The Depression Initiative. In the support group, we shared our stories with each other, and we learned coping mechanisms to help us deal with the trauma. Linda made time to see me a lot outside of group therapy, and she worked diligently trying to resolve my issues. She held on to my journals and reached out to my friends and family and my children to try to open a door to communication when I was at my lowest. She made some headway and gleaned some information from those phone calls with some of my kids that helped sustain me for a little while, but the main thing I needed was to become part of my children's lives again. This is something the doctors wouldn't attempt, saying I needed to heal myself first. Linda went out of her way to try to open up those lines of communication with my children. I remember so many times visiting her at her house at Musselman's Lake and just doing some gardening and talking or sitting in the kitchen making lunch or visiting with friends who were supportive and were trying to help me.

Linda took it upon herself to invite a group of my old friends and a group of my new friends to sit together at her house and try to find a way to support me in my quest to find hope. She is the one responsible for starting the Christmas and Thanksgiving dinners for trans people at our church, for anyone who was spending the holidays alone and for those who would support us during those difficult times. Linda was a part of the filming of *Paul Wears Dresses* and witnessed the backlash from trolls responding to the *Xtra* interview. She stayed with me so many times when I was scared and managed to clarify what I was and wasn't in control of and help me move forward from all that trauma. Linda was there until I left the church in 2018 because my depression had got the worst of me. Five years later, I would go back to MCCT, and she and the clergy were there to welcome me back and celebrate the good news that my children and brothers were back in my life.

I was excited to be back at MCC Toronto because a lot had changed, and I had a lot to be thankful for. I had re-established my connection with four of my kids and six of my grandchildren, which was the miracle I needed to help overcome my worst depression and anxiety. Now Linda is helping me write this book and patiently editing every chapter that I have just barfed out to get it done. We work well together, and we have discussed so many different ways of saying what needs to be said.

I've made a lot of friends at church who show me love and acceptance. I have found a true spiritual home at MCC Toronto, and I feel strong enough to start giving back to the church family that has stuck by me throughout the worst of times. Thank you, everyone, for praying for me.

I still struggle with disappointments, just like everyone else, but they don't trigger me to the point where I need to go into the crisis unit. I am able to think things through with a clear mind and deduce that everything will be good again sooner or later. I have found hope, and with hope comes healing. So now I believe I'm on that path of healing to become a better version of myself, free from all this baggage and isolation.

I've also made a lot of friends during my stays in the hospital, crisis units, and in group therapy. These friends are woven into the fabric of my life and bring me fond memories of working through mental issues together. I can't tell you all the names of everyone who helped make my stay in the hospital so amazingly therapeutic. But there is one person, Allison Hannaford, that I need to acknowledge.

Allison and I met at CAMH when I was at my worst. I had been meeting with a therapist who knew what my triggers were and, despite its setting me back, kept asking me over and over to explain how my relationship with my children, or lack thereof, triggered me to want to kill myself. One day, while I was in a therapy session, I was crying and staring out the window, trying to answer his questions, when I suddenly lost my voice. I had to write down on a piece of paper that he was pushing me too hard, which led to him sending me to the emergency ward on a form one. I was really feeling like everything was hopeless. While in the crisis unit, they put me in a room where the fluorescent lights wouldn't turn off. This was a trigger for me, and I begged them to turn off the lights or get maintenance to take the light bulbs out because when I was in solitary confinement for nine days, the guards left the lights on day and night. I think it was the fluorescent lights that slowly drove me crazy because incandescent lights don't trigger me.

After that outburst, I was sent up to the women's floor at CAMH, where I met Allison, and we soon became friends. Everyone on that floor, patients and nurses alike, seem to work as a team to make everyone feel safe.

Allison and I continued being friends long after we left the hospital. We would visit each other, console each other, and support each other through the good times and the bad.

Mykoto-kun and Stefonknee (November 2023)

Allison and I shared a cat, Mykoto-kun, who would be shuffled between our apartments whenever one of us needed to be admitted to the hospital.

Allison and I could talk about everything—our families and life stories. It's nice that Allison and I both started doing better at the same time. For her, it was going back to school and getting her degree in journalism. Allison has been extremely successful in her

245

career and has taken time to mentor me with my writing and to help me complete this book.

For me, getting back together with my children was what I needed to start moving forward with family relationships that helped me overcome depression and make life worth living. Long before that happened, there was another important relationship that helped make my life bearable.

Chapter 17
Adrian Field, 2014

It was a freezing spring day on March 31, 2014, when I met Adrian Field, a man who would soon become my boyfriend and take the role of my "Daddy." He was in a polyamorous relationship with his girlfriend, and she was aware of him communicating with me on the internet. In fact, she and I exchanged phone numbers. One day in late March, Adrian came down to Toronto and took me out for lunch and to the club to just hang out.

While walking to the restaurant, in the middle of Yonge Street, he asked me, "So what do you think?"

I responded with, "I think I'm in love."

We chatted over lunch, and the whole time I had butterflies in my stomach. It was so easy to talk to Adrian. We went on to have a great time at a club that afternoon but eventually, it was time to say goodbye. He went back up to Peterborough, and I went back to my apartment on Pembroke Street.

Adrian Field (March 2015)

Holding On by a Thread

Once back in my apartment, I called Serena, his girlfriend, to let her know how the afternoon had gone. It wouldn't be long before I would be heading up to Peterborough to meet with the two of them in his house on a regular basis.

Up in Peterborough, we had a great relationship. There were the ups and downs, but they differed from what I had experienced with my wife. I think, for the first time, I was in love with someone other than my children and grandchildren. We went out on dates as a threesome quite often, enjoying local establishments and going to the lake for a swim whenever it got too hot in the summer. I loved spending time in their big backyard filled with flowers and bushes of every kind. I would relax in the hammock and just watch the clouds go by; it was really calm and quiet up there, so different from all the noise in the city.

Adrian supported me through my best of times and my worst of times. He and Serena were both there to take me to the hospital in Peterborough if I was triggered and the play therapy wouldn't work. Quite often, playing in the house or backyard was enough to get me back on my feet, but there were numerous occasions when I had fallen so deep into despair that I needed to be hospitalized. I got to meet their neighbours and Serena's kids and grandkids, and we all hit it off really well. It was pretty amazing having my apartment in Toronto, having a couple who accepted me into their life as a little girl in Peterborough, and their relatives who enjoyed exploring the vast expanse of my imagination and my humour when I was feeling good, and who were sympathetic with my suffering when I wasn't feeling so great.

Adrian and Stefonknee (September 14, 2017)

I like to think that I should fit in despite my being a trans woman, and Peterborough is one of those places where I've always felt welcome. Quite often, as a trans woman, there are no opportunities to contribute to society because no one sees you as a person because they can't see past your gender identity. This isn't true for Peterborough. I feel like my identity is no different from anyone else's and I am well respected by residents. I can be useful in Peterborough.

While up in Peterborough, I often took on tasks around the house repairing stuff. My biggest task was waterproofing the basement because there was frost damage to the basement walls.

Alan Cavers helping me repair the basement in Peterborough "It's go time!" (April, 2017)

One year, when Adrian and Serena had gone to Florida for vacation, I started a plan to fix their basement as a parting gift, should I pass away, to thank them for being there for me. With the help of their neighbour, Alan, and his son-in-law, Trevor, we excavated the ground around the house and found multiple holes that had allowed water to seep into the foundation walls. While digging, we also found a staircase buried under the deck with a haphazardly sealed-off doorway to the basement from the outside. There were just loose bricks and blocks closing the hole, and there was no waterproofing or protection from the outside elements. The frost had also destroyed the foundation of the rear deck, so we needed to demolish that, too.

Finished deck and backyard in Peterborough, ON. (May 2017)

Adrian had emigrated to Canada from England, and I consider myself really lucky to have found him. He is my rock and he taught me that I was lovable. He has a beautiful British accent and a great sense of humor. (He's also really good at letting me know when to expect to work plowing snow, as he's an amateur meteorologist and is constantly checking weather maps.) He also loves trains more than anyone I've ever met before. I'm really glad he came into my life when he did because he helped me through some very tough times.

Just before Covid-19 happened, I had a falling out with Serena, and I would be separated from Adrian for the next two and a half years. Since May of 2023, Adrian and I are back together because Serena left him for another man and got married. Adrian and I are best friends. We love each other's company and are there to support each other in good times and in bad. I couldn't imagine my life without him; he has taught me what real love and understanding are and accepts me unconditionally. He was there for me when I was on trial and in jail. He never judged me and trusted in me when I was persecuted.

When I go up and visit him, we spend countless hours together just being friends and talking about some of the hardships in our lives. Not only do I appreciate going up to his home to relax but my cat, Mykoto-kun, has grown fond of Adrian as well, and loves being at his house, despite meowing all the way up in the car and all the way home as well.

Adrian's cousin Mark and his wife, Karen, have accepted me and become really good friends. I can't go visiting up there without the four of us going out for dinner to catch up on everything that has changed and reminisce about the past. Mark and Karen are very supportive of me as a trans woman and advocate on my behalf to the rest of their family, who support me as well.

Adrian has stuck by me, and I can't imagine spending the rest of my life with anyone else. I really love him.

I'm still friends with his neighbours Alan and Carol, and Gloria across the road, who is now a widow as Paul passed away a year ago. Gloria has amazing kids who help her cope with the isolation of being a widow.

I can't tell you enough good things about Peterborough; the people up there are very good at letting me, a trans woman, feel welcome and safe. On numerous occasions, I have been stopped and introduced to people who are either trans themselves or know someone who is transgender.

I've marched in the Peterborough Pride Parade several times, and it has always been an amazing experience for a community with so many senior citizens. There is a real sense of pride because they embrace the LGBTQ+ community up there.

I feel honored to have Peterborough as a second home where I can get away from all the noise of the city and enjoy the quiet of being out in the country.

Chapter 18

Paul Wears Dresses, 2014

At the beginning of June 2014, I was approached by Kevin O'Keefe of Stornoway Media Corp. He asked if I would consider doing a documentary about my life as a trans woman, and after some consideration, I said yes. We would meet regularly to discuss locations and scenarios and decide on the title *Paul Wears Dresses*.

On June 26, 2014, we began filming. The filming started at the Trans March during World Pride in Toronto. They noted that I was missing from the march that year and it had to do with the politics that I mentioned earlier in the book and Pride Toronto's disrespect for the trans community. After filming on Yonge Street, the crew came to my backyard and started interviewing me, enjoying the sun and shade on a beautiful day in the privacy of our cozy backyard.

That same day, they filmed me doing some auto repair work on my friend Melissa Rhind's car in the back parking lot in a dress. The next thing that we had scheduled was a road trip to Mount Albert.

Up in Mount Albert, we visited our old farms, first going to the back of our second farm, called "The 11A," and filming in the park area. I was wearing a yellow dress and enjoying the breeze of a nice, warm day. It was there that we decided that I'd like it to be called *Paul Wears Dresses*.

It was important for me to have that title because I had spent forty-six years being Paul and putting on dresses to express my feminine side. By saying my name and acknowledging that I wear dresses, it destroyed all those years of doing it in secret. I was coming out to the world to say *this is me, and I love my dresses*.

After filming at The 11A, we went to our home farm, which was no longer there, long since replaced by a subdivision of houses. We drove into our old driveway and did some footage of me walking around in the exact area where the trauma happened to me when I was four years old. The same trees still stand there, although the forts are gone.

Afterwards, while the crew was packing up their equipment, I took a moment to go to say hi to Dean and Brian at Mount Albert Auto Repair. Dean and Brian are a couple years older than I am, and they've been mechanics since they left high school—just like me. The film crew quickly grabbed their equipment and began filming again. We bantered about our childhood, about the recent fire at the Mount Albert Fire Hall, and talked about my wearing dresses and what had happened. Dean and Brian were very comfortable with me standing there in a dress and we shook hands and said our goodbyes after so many years of being estranged. I left there thinking *all is well, and all is well, in all manner of things, all is well.*

Holding On by a Thread

The film was released in November 2014. By December, Kevin was no longer working at Stornoway but was now working for *Xtra* magazine. He called me to ask if I would come in and be interviewed about the making of *Paul Wears Dresses*. I agreed and went to *Xtra* for the interview the following Wednesday. The interview went well: it was recorded in their video control room with all the monitors and lights constantly changing. While being interviewed, I also interjected about my using play therapy to help me cope with my depression when I'm in crisis and thought nothing more of it.

That comment made the interview go viral around the world, with over a million views in the first two days. I remember it was the weekend, and I was amazed at how much attention it received and how much attention was focused on my using play therapy to help me avoid going into crisis. By Monday, the interview had 1.2 million views and I had over 900 death threats. It seemed like everyone picked up on the fact that I like to be a six-year-old girl and that they assumed I lived as a six-year-old all the time. I knew it had gone viral because my apartment superintendent, Vivian, called me from her vacation in Greece, telling me I was all over the news.

This is probably a good spot to talk about all the hate that's out there towards me.

257

All over the world, various media wrote stories because of half-truths about me leaving my children and wife to pursue a life as a six-year-old girl. After reading this far, I hope you can see that my reasons for leaving were quite different and that my reason for identifying as a six-year-old girl on occasion was therapeutic. I have to admit, at first, when it happened, I was extremely triggered and frightened when I got over 900 death threats. Although most of them have been deleted, they scared me, and I feared for my life.

It's kind of weird fearing for your life when you're suicidal. The only way I can explain it is I didn't want to be walking around as a living target waiting for someone to shoot or stab me; I wanted to die on my terms. Unfortunately, the trolls and the haters out there couldn't wait to profit off the lies. Truth doesn't sell very well, and the lies were more dramatic, especially when they added the word *pedophile* to my profile. I often wonder if these haters have internalized transphobia and they're turned on by the public profile that has been created.

Quite often, the people who hate homosexuals or trans people are themselves homosexual or trans, but they try so hard to protect their own secret that they attack the very people who identify the same as them. I believe that out of all my haters, probably half of them are closeted age-players or closeted transgender people. Why else would they take so much time to follow me and interact with me? Some of them go on and on about what they think of what

I'm doing. What's that saying? "The lady doth protest too much, methinks."

I don't hate the people who write nasty stuff about me because I believe it's a barometer of where the world is at this time. When they first started writing it, people were still calling our human rights campaign a "bathroom bill," and here we are nine years later, and nothing has happened in women's bathrooms. Today, more people are supportive in the comment section of my posts than they were ten years ago. So, I've left those nasty comments up as a sign of where we were in the past. I no longer fear for my life, the haters have done their worst, and it ended up just being all talk and no action. I've never been attacked by any of those people who had threatened to kill me online. The people who have attacked me are usually drunk and in a gang.

Unfortunately, people did threaten me in December of 2014, and I was triggered by those death threats at the time. This is what led up to my becoming a missing person and going into hiding.

"Mommy and Daddy," Serena and Adrian, were down in Florida, and I was checking their house and plants for them, so I drove up to Peterborough, put my car in the garage, went down into the basement, and turned off all the lights. I called a friend of mine, Andrea, who worked at *Xtra* as a reporter and told her that I couldn't handle the pressure and that it was pushing me to the brink of suicide. Andrea panicked, and a few hours later, I got a phone call in the middle of the night from my friend Kathy asking me if I was okay because I was on the television as a missing person.

I ended up going to the Peterborough police station and telling them what had happened. I filled out a report, after which they told me to go home and stay out of sight and that an officer and a social worker would come by in the morning to help me walk through the next steps. The next morning came and went, and nobody came to my door. I waited the whole day and by evening, I took the battery out of my cell phone and headed back to Toronto, still fearing for my life. I left my vehicle in front of my house and hitched a ride to my friend Jeffrey's house, where we spent the night scanning the dark web to see what was being said about me all over the world. From there, I called my friend Robin, who was the LGBT liaison at St. Mike's Hospital, and she arranged to get me a bed in the crisis unit where I would be safe. When I got to the hospital, she met me and told me that all the paperwork was done and to follow her so I could get some sleep.

The next day at noon, I was discharged, much calmer, and no longer feeling like a hunted rabbit, afraid to peek out of the ground with my heart racing. So, I went online and told anyone that wanted to kill me to meet me at Allan Gardens by the statue at one p.m., and I would be there for them to do as they pleased. My life felt hopeless and to be honest, at that point, I just wanted to die.

When I got to the statue just before one, a few of the deacons and a pastor from MCCT were there waiting for me and asked me to go with them. I declined the invitation and said I would wait for someone to come and kill me. None of the cowards showed up, and an hour later, I went home feeling much safer. One of these idiots actually messaged me to say he was busy that day and if I could go back the next day at one p.m., he would come to kill me then.

I responded with, "What could you be so busy with that you wouldn't come out to kill somebody? If you seriously wanted to kill me, I'm sure you would have put everything else on the back burner because you'd be going to prison anyway."

Journalists and podcasters started calling me from around the world to interview me and get my side of the story, which was good. It gave me a chance to correct the message that was sent out because of the way the *Xtra* interview was edited. I explained to them that I was only six when I was in crisis. Through radio talk shows in Ireland, Australia, and the USA, interviews with newspapers throughout Canada and the UK, and all the podcasters throughout the internet, my message had reached the world. Maybe thinking and playing like a child will help people who are in crisis get back to a safe place. I hope that play therapy for adults as a legitimate form of therapy for depression will someday be studied by doctors.

In addition to all these interviews, I was given the opportunity to make two more documentaries, one for a television station in Europe that would be televised in Germany, Austria, and Switzerland, and another by Nippon Media Corporation in Japan, the equivalent of our CBC, ABC, or BBC.

Along with these legitimate media sources, I was inundated with videos made by internet trolls and TERFs (Trans Exclusionary Radical Feminists). TERFs like the woman who goes by the name "Gallus Mag," went to extreme measures to attack the transgender community, and trans women in particular for invading women's spaces and identities. You just need to Google my name, "Stefonknee," to see all the hate. These responses act as a litmus test to see how society accepts trans people. The internet is awash with hate.

I learned two things from all this media attention: the first is that you can never trust that what you've said will be presented in the final production of a video. The second is that a lot of haters out there on the internet are looking for a reason to promote anger and hatred towards people they don't even know. Now that I've found hope in my life, I regret letting that negative news change who I was.

Chapter 19
Playtime and "Bertha"

Throughout my homelessness, starting in 2009, I've been shown many ways to cope with depression, anxiety, and suicidal thoughts. I tried CBT (Cognitive Behavioural Therapy) and DBT (Dialectical Behavioural Therapy) and I found that often they didn't help me at all. In fact, they were triggers—different, unexpected things that made my anxiety and depression worse—and on many occasions, I had to leave the therapy meetings and be sent to the hospital.

I enjoyed doing art therapy with Carol Baker in the beginning until she retired. Then I started going to the VanDuzer art studio, a quaint carriage house behind one of the shelters in Toronto on Beverley Street, where students from OCAD University (Ontario College of Art and Design) taught various kinds of art. There was always a different group of people with mental health challenges, all of them friendly, inclusive, and approachable.

Later, I joined the support group at St. Michael's Hospital as well. It was really well organized, with refreshments and a nice meeting room, a facilitator and support staff, but somehow, it seemed very superficial. I was never able to just let my guard down and share what I needed to talk about. I spent most of the time listening to other people go on about their situations, and in my mind, I would just distance myself from everybody in the room. I stuck with it for a while, but unfortunately, the sharing started to trigger me, so I decided to leave the group.

I also joined the depression group held at MCC Toronto, led by Linda Leenders, where we learned many ways of coping with depression and how to reprogram our minds to avoid triggers. Linda was very kind and always supportive of everyone in the group. She always had coffee and tea available and would make a healthy homemade soup, which reminded me of my mom. This felt like a place where I could really trust everyone and share my deepest fears. Linda took me under her wing and helped me throughout the years. The help that I received at MCCT got me through some of the darkest days of my life and kept me safe.

Ella, Franny and Lily

Something else that happened to me throughout this ordeal, starting with Vermilion Fire and carrying on throughout the years, was play therapy, where I got to be a little girl for the first time in my life. I started going on playdates with a friend named Seven. Her real name was Sarah, and she would have house parties where other people who used play as therapy, called "littles," would come and we would make a snack like cupcakes and decorate them, enjoy ice cream, and do crafts, as well as watch cartoons on her TV and play on her couch and floor like little kids. This was so liberating, as it allowed us to release our inner child and it let us free ourselves from the traumas that we brought with us to the party. Sarah and I would often go shopping before each party to pick up the supplies and then we would prepare her house for all the visitors. Slowly, they would all trickle in, get changed, and be little kids, both little girls and little boys. I was the only transgender person there. After the party at her house, we would all travel downtown and have dinner at the Church Mouse pub in the gay village.

At one of the dinners, a couple of guys who were littles were bragging about their pickup trucks and their four-wheelers and all the alpha male stuff that they had and loved. They didn't want me talking about play therapy in public and they complained to Sarah that I was outing them, when, in reality, we were in the village, and we were safe. Sarah called me that night to tell me that I had to be more careful about what I said at the table, even though we were secluded in the back corner of the restaurant behind the kitchen.

I was triggered by this, and I went to the establishment's owners to ask them if it was a problem talking about playtime in the restaurant. They assured me that we'd spent too long in the closet to have anyone try to push us back in by censoring our speech in the village, which was in my neighborhood. The owner suggested that they might consider having their dinners in Oshawa if they wanted to do that kind of censorship. I called Sarah and let her know that the owners of the restaurant didn't see a problem with what we were doing there, but they suggested that if we want to talk about pickup trucks and four-wheelers, that we go to a restaurant in Oshawa. She didn't like that response, so that was the last time I went to a littles party at Sarah's house.

Other friends of mine, Kathy and Belle, have a house up in Scarborough with a heated saltwater pool in the backyard. Belle was a little for a long time, too, until he outgrew it. Kathy was totally into inviting littles over for pool parties with crafts and treats, and her annual Halloween party was always a blast. Kathy, Belle, and I became really good friends over the years.

Stefonknee in Kathy and Belle's pool (July 2019)

Eventually, I found the couple, Serena and Adrian, in Peterborough, who would become my Mommy and Daddy. They knew I was transgender, and they knew I was an eight-year-old girl when I was age playing. They accepted me for who I was. It was at this point that Serena's seven-year-old granddaughter wanted to be nine so I could be her little sister. Rather than that, I suggested she stay seven and I changed my age to six to accommodate her having me as a little sister.

When I was up in Peterborough, I had my own bedroom with Mickey and Minnie Mouse, Pippi Longstocking, Donald Duck, and Goofy painted on the walls. In my bedroom, I had my colouring books, a desk, and all my dresses hung neatly in the closet. I would bring my dolls with me, and we would have play time whenever Mommy and Daddy thought it was important for me to relax and deal with my anxiety and depression.

I would often take care of things outside the house, such as cleaning the garage, cutting the grass, or raking the leaves. Once, I was raking the leaves in the front yard in a little play dress on a windy day when the new neighbours across the road had their children and grandchildren come over for Thanksgiving dinner. I didn't know it at the time, but they were watching me in my pretty dress doing yard work in the wind. The next day, I went over to meet them. I introduced myself to Paul and Gloria, who accepted me as I was and told me that their grandchildren and children were fascinated by me dressed the way I was and raking leaves in the wind. They did not judge me, they did not make me feel guilty. They just thought it was great and they loved getting to know me as a neighbour.

The other neighbours on the left and the right of the property also were fine with my dressing and being a little. The neighbours to the south of us, Alan and Carol, would often chat with me over the fence. One day, Alan was sitting on his front porch, and he offered me a drink, so I came over and sat down and chatted with him. He confided that he appreciated getting to know me and realizing that I was just another person—different from him, but a nice person who wore dresses and played in the backyard—because it helped him to better understand his own adult children and decisions that they made in their lives, that he was not sure about. He'd become more accepting of them. He was a man's man who liked to play hockey, go fishing and hunting, and do all the guy stuff, but he appreciated my being a mechanic despite my wearing dresses.

One day, we were working in his backyard, and his whole family was there; the kids were visiting from out of town. Carol asked, "Is there any way that we could take the Christmas lights down?" because it was the middle of summer and she had been bugging Alan to take them down since January.

I told her that it was perhaps the way she was asking him to take them down and could I try to rephrase the request? She told me to go ahead and try, so I told Alan that the Christmas lights made his house look like a gay bar, upon which he reached up and pulled the lights down. We all had a good laugh.

After being accepted by so many people, I felt very safe expressing my "little" side, and I took every opportunity to share how play therapy works for me.

I have since created a website http://Stefonknee.com for other people to meet and chat about being sissies and using age play or play therapy and just being little to help get through the tough times.

I love being a little, I love my dolls, I love my teddy bears, I love coloring, and I love puzzles. All the little girl things that I couldn't do as a child I was now free to entertain as an adult, and this was liberating and a great way for me to expand the definition of who I really was.

To respond to the negative publicity, I made a few videos that showed me being a little for my YouTube channel. These videos were my way of letting these people know that I was not intimidated by their death threats. In fact, if anything, I wanted to show them that I was more determined than ever to promote play therapy as a form of adult therapy to deal with anxiety and depression.

I don't know if this was the best thing for me to do; perhaps I should have just remained quiet and turned off the comment section of my videos, but by the time I realized how much negative attention I was getting since the *Xtra* interview there wasn't a whole lot I could do anymore. It was out of my control.

One positive thing that happened because of this backlash was that the human rights campaign had evidence of the vile hatred towards me as a trans person and as a little, and people around the world were getting the message through television, radio, and newspaper articles talking about what was happening in Toronto. Bill Siksay, the federal MP who was presenting Bill C-16, came to interview me in Toronto, to talk about the hatred that I was experiencing. In the end we were successful in getting human rights inclusion.

Another thing that happened in the summer of 2014 was that I saw a video on YouTube of a snowplow driving around a Walmart parking lot without an operator. Someone had started the tractor, put it in gear, jumped out, and let it go around in circles, smashing into cars, the store building, and trees. I suspect the person who put the video on YouTube is probably the same person who started this catastrophe. I recognized the logo on the tractor and contacted the company to see if they needed an extra driver, which they did not find funny, but they did agree that they could use more help.

Because I'd been homeless for five years, I knew my resume was worthless, but I had more than ten years' experience operating that machine in the Newmarket area. There was nothing I could do other than to ask for a key and let them see me drive the tractor and plow and show them what I could do. With that in mind, I went up for an interview and spoke to Nino and Nate in Markham. The meeting went really well: we laughed and reminisced about past storms and the amount of stress and pressure on a business like theirs to step up and show results when the big storms came.

At the interview, I led with the fact that I'd seen the video, and it looked like they were one operator short. The owner of the company did not find that funny and mentioned that the perpetrators had never been caught. But he hired me, which was the beginning of my relationship with the property maintenance company Fore North operating under the name Clintar, working part-time in the winter. They offered me a fair starting wage, making me accept their offer immediately. I started working that November. I've had a lot of great experiences with them over the past ten years and really enjoy driving the tractor that I named "Bertha" and plowing snow. They've been more than fair to me, and I love working for them.

Bertha, my snow shovel. (December 2019)

I should also add that they have accepted me as a trans woman and refer to me as Stefonknee. They have hired more trans people throughout the years, and everyone says nothing but good things about them: all of the crew members treat us respectfully and respect our pronouns. It's a real adrenaline rush to get out there in a snowstorm behind the wheel of a 6150 John Deere with a sixteen-foot plow on it and move the snow effortlessly across the parking lots. It's especially fun getting to be my little self while plowing snow.

Chapter 20
Arrest #3, March 2015

On March 1, 2015, I was visiting my friend, Melissa Rhind, watching *The Sound of Music,* and I remember crying as I sang along to the songs that I used to sing with my kids. The phone rang and it was someone at my building on Pembroke named Patrick. He said he was coming over to visit me and asked if I could come home. I thought it was Patrick from our church, and I invited him to come over to Melissa's house and join us in watching *The Sound of Music.* He insisted that I meet him at my apartment, so I asked Melissa if she would mind driving me home so I could find out what was going on.

As we rounded the corner, I saw three police cars on the street and found police standing outside my door. They were there to arrest me but didn't tell me why. I was hustled away in the backseat of a cruiser and taken up to the York Region police station in Richmond Hill. The officer assigned to my case was David Ayette. As soon as I got there, one of the police officers forced me to sit down, and at the same time, a desk clerk asked me to come up to the desk and sign some papers. I got up to sign the papers and the first officer yelled at me to sit back down. I looked them in the eye and said, "Your buddy wants me to sign some papers, so fuck off."

I think at that point, he knew I really didn't care what they were up to. I signed the papers and then another officer came up to me to ask me if I wanted a male or female officer to do the strip search, at which point I just took off all my clothes and stood there naked in front of everyone. I refuse to let them get under my skin, literally.

They told me to put my clothes back on, which I refused to do and then they led me down the hall to a holding cell where I was by myself, alone, naked, and frustrated. Sometime during the night, they brought me some food, which I threw into the toilet. I spent the night alone and naked in my cell while being watched by two CCTV cameras. I hated this game they played, disrupting my life because of their personal insecurities about my being transgender. Still, I'd be damned if they would get any satisfaction out of scaring me this time.

The next morning, they asked me to get dressed to go to court. I refused and the transport vehicle left without me. They made it sound urgent, that I needed to get dressed and be on my way and kept coming to my cell to ask me why I wouldn't get dressed.

I told them I was tired of their stupid games. Eventually, they said they would take me up in a cruiser if I would get dressed and it was getting close to noon, so I got dressed and went with them up to the courthouse in Newmarket.

Once I arrived and was processed and put into a holding cell, I was forgotten about. The entire day was a waste of time; no judge had time to see me, and I wasn't about to be released. Instead, I was shackled and handcuffed again and taken by a transport vehicle up to the Central East Detention Center in Lindsay. Once up in Lindsay, I could hear someone in the transport van crying, so I told them to wipe their tears away and stop showing weakness. "It'll only make things worse." I then said that I had three words of advice for them. "Beetlejuice, Beetlejuice, Beetlejuice."

As soon as I finished saying that, my door opened and I thanked God that it wasn't a sandworm but rather a guard, who then escorted me into the facility. Once inside, the receiving officer took me into her office and told me that she wasn't sure how to fill out paperwork for transgender people. I took a look at the forms and assured her that I had helped draft up these papers, and that I could help her fill them out. She appreciated the help, and as a favor to me, she looked up Adrian's phone number and wrote it down for me so I could call him and let him know that I had been arrested again.

I called Adrian and told him not to worry, that I was in custody in Lindsay and that I would let them know if anything changed. Shortly after making the phone call, they brought me some food, some kind of yellow stuff, a sandwich, and some red liquid in a plastic bag. Again, I was not hungry, so I pushed it aside. It had now been twenty-four hours since I'd eaten or drunk anything. They took me down the hall to be strip searched again and had me change into jail clothes, a disgusting green tracksuit covered in hair and shoes that were four sizes too big. They took away my dress and that would be the last time I ever saw that dress. I was led down a couple of corridors to a holding cell in segregation and after I was put in my cell, I was left there for the night.

In the cell, there was a four-inch-wide window running vertically from floor to ceiling that was deep enough into the wall that I couldn't see anything to the left or right, just a bright spotlight in the yard. The spotlight was shining directly into that window, so I couldn't tell if it was day or night. Like before, this cell also had a fluorescent light that would never get turned off and a freezing cold bed. I ended up trying to sleep with the light on, with only a thin, hairy blanket, my tracksuit and shoes on to try to stay warm. I couldn't fall asleep; it was too cold. I paced the room and counted the blocks on the wall. I can't remember how many there were, but I remember those concrete blocks and a steel door kept me from freedom.

The next morning, they brought me food, and I told them I was not going to eat until I was released and that I would be on a hunger strike, to fight against the use of time served plus a day.

Something the legal system does to get a guilty plea is to offer to release you and drive you home with your belongings if you just plead guilty. That's called *time served plus a day*. If you choose to defend yourself, you must find your way from court in Newmarket back up to Lindsay, a ninety-minute drive away, without your cell phone, money, or your keys. It's very tempting just to give in, plead guilty, and just go home. This makes their statistics look better because more of the people that they arrest are found guilty of something, anything to justify the arrests.

In Lindsay, they wouldn't put me into the general population, so instead, I would spend the next nine days in segregation. Someone did come and talk to me about my sexual preferences and upon hearing that I was bisexual, they made the decision to keep me segregated. Because I wouldn't eat their food, they took away my yard privileges and my shower privileges.

With only a small rubber toothbrush, a comb, and a short pencil, I spent my days sketching on the ceiling, brushing my teeth, and pacing my room. When I came in on the first day, they took out my nose stud, so to stop it from closing up, I broke one of the bristles off the comb and stuck it into the piercing in my nose.

The next day, I asked for Cheri DiNovo's phone number. (She was the MPP who'd introduced Toby's Act, an act to defend transgender rights within Ontario, that had passed into law and was why they had the new paperwork I needed to fill out upon arriving at the jail.) The guard laughed at me and said no MPP would waste their time with someone like me. They did get me the number but wouldn't bring my phone to my cell. Through the little hatch that flopped down, that they would put the food trays on, I had to call collect on a payphone. Except for the top three numbers, the rest were hidden by the flap in the door, so prisoners had to get accustomed to dialing without seeing the keys.

The guards refused to bring me the phone because the woman in the cell to my left was defending herself and didn't speak a word of English but needed the phone to make her defence. I looked through the slot in the door and saw that she was pressing the five button over and over again, which meant she wasn't calling anyone. She was just speaking in Chinese to the dial tone.

Once she stopped talking on the phone, the guards brought it to my door. After four or five failed attempts, I got through to Queens Park, and to my amazement, my friend Andrea Houston answered the phone. She was now working at Queen's Park and agreed to accept the charges. I yelled *Andrea, is this really you? What are you doing there? You're not going to believe where I am.*

I was so excited to finally talk to someone that I knew, and I told her everything that had happened, that I still didn't know why I was in jail but that they were keeping me in Lindsay at the Central East Detention Center. She assured me that she would let Cheri DiNovo know, and she would let people know that I was on a hunger strike for time served plus a day.

My friend Judy Ruzylo and her partner David York offered to pay a lawyer to defend me. We had just finished filming a documentary called *Happy Birthday Tammy Moone*, telling the story of Tammy and my transition. This lawyer, Jeffrey David Ayette, came to talk to me about accepting a plea deal. He explained to me that I was charged with uttering death threats, and they could work something out to let me go home in the morning. I told him I was not guilty and would not plead guilty just to get out of this mess. I told him that I was now their problem and they had to figure out what to do with me. I couldn't help but wonder if Jeffrey David Ayette was any relation to the arresting officer, David Ayette.

For the first couple of days, not eating and drinking was easy. I met with a social worker and a psychiatrist the next morning, who seemed friendly enough, and they were concerned about my mental health and my not eating. I assured them that I was okay and that I would eat once I was free. While in that room with the social worker and psychiatrist, a guard came to say that I was to stand in a room with a TV and a microphone to talk to a judge. I had done that years before, and it was a shit show, so I refused and told the guard to tell the judge that I was busy in therapy.

The guard became quite upset and warned me that I would be held in contempt of court if I did not go and appear before the judge.

I said, "You've already got me in segregation without any privileges and I'm not eating your food. What more could you possibly do to me?"

Later that night, the guards came and told me that I had guests and I needed to go to the visiting area. They led me down a bunch of corridors to a small room with a telephone and a glass window, and a few minutes later, Adrian and Serena showed up. They said that they had got a call from a newspaper about my being incarcerated and if they should give them any information. I told them to call the newspaper and let them know that I was on a hunger strike to protest time served plus a day. We chatted for a while, said our goodbyes, and I let them know that I still loved them despite being a criminal.

That night, I did get a bit of sleep, but my lips started to chap as it had now been three days since I'd had anything to drink, and I was starting to feel the effects of dehydration. I was surprised that I still had to go pee on a regular basis since I wasn't drinking anything, but it must have been my kidneys draining out the toxins from my body.

By day three, I was asked by two OPP (Ontario Provincial Police) officers to get into a transport van to go down to Newmarket court to go before a judge. I asked them to get my belongings and bring them along just in case I was released because I had no way of getting back up to Lindsay if I got bail in Newmarket that day. They refused to take my purse and my clothes in the transport van, so I refused to go with them. This agitated them and they let me know it.

About an hour later, two guards came to my cell and told me that they would take me to Newmarket in a van and they would bring my belongings with us. Shortly after that, I was strip searched and changed into a clean purple tracksuit, which was for the public to see. Along the way to the courthouse, the guards stopped at Tim Hortons and asked me if I wanted anything. At first, I refused, but as we were going through the drive-thru I asked them if I could get a large, regular coffee, please. They were nice to me, and this was the first thing that I had to drink in four days. I was brought down to Newmarket and put in a holding cell that was freezing cold. The guy in the cell to the right of me could not speak very good English and he kept saying something like "code, code," which I took to mean that he wanted his coat because it was cold, and it was really cold. When lunch came around, I told the guards that I was not eating, so they passed me by. The guy in the next cell took a sandwich and said, "More, more," but the guards told them just one sandwich per inmate. So, as they walked by my cell again, I told them I had changed my mind and I would eat a sandwich, so they gave me a sandwich, which I handed to Mr "more, more," once they were out of sight.

I was still on the hunger strike even though I had that one cup of coffee. By this point, it was past three in the afternoon and I knew that there was no chance of me seeing a judge, and I wasn't feeling well. My head began to spin, my heart was racing, and I was having really bad acid reflux. When the guards came to drive me back up to Lindsay, I told them, "I think I need to see a doctor. Can we stop at the hospital?"

They called for a paramedic who came and took my vitals and told them that we needed to go to a hospital and get me some fluids because I was extremely dehydrated. The two cops detoured over to the Newmarket Hospital, where I was given the choice to either eat crushed ice or be put on an intravenous drip. I lay in the bed chewing on ice while the two guards joked about needing to handcuff me so I wouldn't run away. In reality, I had difficulty standing up because I was so weak.

Back up in Lindsay, I started pushing the emergency button in my room because I was tired of being in segregation and I needed to know what time it was. With the lights on all the time, isolated in my cell, I had no contact with anything resembling normal and no concept of time. Two guards, one very tall and one very short, came across the corridor, screaming at me for pushing the emergency button. I told them that I needed to know what time it was, and they told me to stop pushing the emergency button, that it was only for emergencies.

I laughed and told them, "I need it to know what time it is, so please just tell me what time it is, and I'll stop."

They refused, so I just kept pushing the emergency button. I knew that they were supposed to check on us every twenty minutes, and they were not doing that. I counted out in my mind what should have been twenty minutes, then thirty minutes, then an hour, then two hours, and no one came to check on us. I was furious. I would later learn in the transport van from other prisoners that the regular guards were on strike, and these were private security guards that they had hired to fill in, who did not know the routine or what our rights were.

I also learned that it had spread through the jail that I was on a hunger strike and why, which gained me the respect of the other prisoners in the general population.

Know that the entire time that I was being held on remand, I was supposed to be considered innocent until proven guilty. The system, from the police to the guards, to the judges, treats you like you're guilty of something, even if they don't have any evidence.

On day four, they took me down to court in the transport van. It must have been -20°C outside and the metal van had no heat in it. They left the truck running until the cab was warm but we were in the back, freezing our butts off. I was sure that I could get frostbite, so I took all my clothes off, removed my shoes, and sat by the doorway, hoping to die. The entire drive down to Newmarket, I was freezing but ten minutes before getting to the courthouse, they turned the heat on in the back. Feeling sick and frustrated, I put my clothes and shoes back on. Again, I sat in a holding cell all day, waiting to go before a judge, only to find out that they had run out of time, and we headed back to Lindsay, having accomplished nothing.

Later that night, I took some toothpaste and smeared it all over the glass in the door that was covered on the outside with a steel door of its own. The next time they did come to check on me, they could not look in, so instead, they had to open the big door to see if I was okay. They told me to clean the toothpaste off the window. I refused to and told them to just knock on the door so that I could keep track of the time and to start checking on me every twenty minutes. I'd let them know that I was alright. That didn't work; they still came whenever they felt like it. When, after shift change, the guards started knocking on my door every twenty minutes, I would make a mark on the wall to keep track of the time. I called it my knock tower clock, and this went on throughout the night.

By day five, the inside of my mouth tasted metallic, my lips were extremely chapped and bleeding, I started feeling pain in my kidneys, and I had trouble standing up. It had now been five days without water or food, just that one cup of coffee and that bit of ice. They brought a medic into my cell, and they checked my vitals, and then gave me some pills to take and a needle to sedate me. When I woke up the next morning, I still refused to eat the food and by noon, they took me to a holding cell where I was to speak to a doctor. When I found out the doctor would be a virtual visit over a television, I asked the guard to take me back to my cell because I refused to be seen virtually. Late that night, they had to take me by ambulance to the hospital again to hydrate me with an intravenous line.

By day seven, I was getting accustomed to the routine of going to court in the morning with my belongings, sitting around all day and not seeing a judge, and being trucked back again to Lindsay. This day was a little different because they actually brought me into a courtroom at three p.m. and had me sit there and wait while the judge did paperwork. Then he began to speak and tell us that he had been in court all day and that he needed to get up and walk around, so he was going to adjourn court for the day. This meant I would be spending the weekend in custody, without any rides to Newmarket in the transport van.

I can't remember too much about the last two days in my cell; all I know is that on Monday morning, they asked me to clean the toothpaste off my window before we left for Newmarket, to which I responded, "I'm not a caretaker; get someone else to do it."

I touched the toothpaste, and it was now hard as a rock. They changed me into the purple tracksuit, and we were whisked off for the ninety-minute drive to Newmarket.

That day, I did see a judge early in the morning, and he told me that if my friends, Adrian and Shadmith, posted $500 bail each, then I would be released on $1,000 bail bond. I told them that I couldn't be responsible for $1,000; it was more than I could afford, and I wouldn't put my friends on the line for that.

The judge asked if I was planning on breaking my bail conditions, to which I responded, "I haven't done anything, and yet you've already thrown me in jail for nine days. How am I to know that you won't do the same thing tomorrow and take their thousand dollars?" I then told the judge that I wouldn't accept five cents bail, that they created this mess, that I'm their problem and they should keep me in custody until the trial. Secretly, I was hoping to die from starvation and dehydration. The judge released me on my own recognizance without any bail conditions.

Adrian and Serena were there in my car, so I drove us home. On the way home, we stopped at Tim Hortons, and I devoured a bagel, some donuts, and a cup of coffee.

All this happened because Kim Sorensen, the person whom I'd invited to live in my apartment for three months, told Arden Ruttan, the guy whom I was supposed to buy the bar with, who told my wife, that I was going to shoot her. What a messed up legal system we have.

Ex friend Kim Sorensen (2014)

After being discharged, I found out that I now had type 2 diabetes. I'm not sure if the hunger strike made it worse but my doctor started me on Metformin. This diagnosis will stay with me for the rest of my life.

Another thing that changed on the day I was arrested: I became asexual. The stress of the ordeal not only caused me to have health issues, but the mental consequences of being asexual have continued to this day, nine years later. This has been an unexpected consequence of that arrest and subsequent trial, a lasting scar.

Originally, my charge was filed as an indictable offense, but when I asked for a jury to judge me for what they were accusing me of, the court changed the documents and had it reduced to a summary offence, which meant it would be heard by a judge. I believed it would be much easier to discriminate against me if it was just one judge, whereas a jury of my peers might empathize with me, and see the trial for what it was, a cruel and sick way to promote hatred towards trans people.

By July 18, 2016, I was finally on trial in front of Justice Misener on the charge of "uttering threats." My anxiety and depression had been out of control since early June, and I'd been hospitalized from June 28 until July 23 at the Peterborough Regional Health Center, medicated for anxiety and depression.

During the year preceding the trial, I was able to get a lawyer, Sean Martinez, who defended me on just legal aid. Sean was kind enough to meet with me at the Law Society of Upper Canada building on Queen Street, in Toronto, so as not to incur extra costs for me, and he constantly brought me up to speed on what he thought would happen in court. He asked that Adrian and Serena be available as witnesses in my defence, as they had witnessed what Kim Sorensen had done prior to her allegations against me.

During the time of my trial, I was allowed to leave the Peterborough hospital on July 18, 19, and 20 to attend court. Adrian and Serena would come to the hospital and sign me out, and I was given enough medication to help control my anxiety for the day. Adrian and Serena were not able to sit in the courtroom to witness what was going on as they were listed as witnesses, although they were never asked to take the stand. My friend Kathy sat through the trial and took rough notes, which she later gave me, but I couldn't make out her handwriting. After the day in court, they would return me back to the hospital, where I would be sedated and sleep till morning.

I was heavily sedated and don't remember anything about the proceedings and court. What I do remember is that my car had developed a rad leak that needed to be fixed on the way home on July 19. I don't know if it was the medication or if I was disassociating but it didn't occur to me that we'd gone to court. Six months later, I called my lawyer to ask if I had forgotten to go to court. Still, he had assured me that we went and on July 20, 2016, I was found not guilty, although Adrian, who was in the court for the verdict, told me that Justice Misener said that if she could find me guilty, she would have sentenced me to thirty years in prison. Where she stood on trans rights was evident from her transphobic comments. While writing this book, it occurred to me that I should get the transcripts from the trial and add an extra chapter about what happened to show how much transphobia is evident at the court in Newmarket and with York Regional Police. I hate the legal system, with the police, lawyers, and judges perpetuating hate and stereotypes about marginalized people. I thank God that Sean Martinez was there to help me through this difficult time.

Chapter 21
Hospital Stays

To say that all of these experiences affected my mental health is an understatement: transitioning from male to female flipped my entire world over those twelve years of my life. From my first visit to Saint Mike's Hospital and being diagnosed with situational depression, complex PTSD, and anxiety, my suicidal ideation was out of control. Triggers were everywhere, from seeing families on the street getting along to the sound of sirens, to being isolated and alone in my apartment. The medication that I was prescribed was not working to keep me safe.

In the last fourteen years, my only hospital visits that weren't for suicidal thoughts were a couple of times to get kidney stones removed, an orchiectomy, and once to x-ray and repair a broken kneecap. My mental health visits for anxiety, depression, and suicidal thoughts would take up the rest of the many hospital admissions, numbering in the dozens. Some of these hospital stays were therapeutic and drew results, but some of them made my situation worse.

One time, I hadn't slept for a couple of days, and I walked down to St. Mike's Hospital to see a crisis nurse in the emergency department. There were two other women in the waiting room, and upon seeing me, one of them picked up her phone and called her daughter to tell her to go straight home and that there were trannies out that night. Even though I was just sitting there quietly crying, she felt like I was a threat to her child.

I ended up seeing an emergency doctor who assessed me and then asked me what I would do if he discharged me? I told him I had everything I needed in my truck to end my life. It was about seven on a Sunday morning, and he discharged me anyway, which meant I had fulfilled my obligation to ask for help.

So, I then went on to try to take my life. I called a lawyer friend and left her a message that told her that she didn't need to keep my file open anymore as I had given up. I then took the battery out of my phone, drove to Cherry Beach, and looked for a low-hanging branch to throw a rope over and kick out the chair that I had brought so as to hang myself. All the branches had been trimmed too high for me to reach, so I ended up putting the rope and the chair back in the truck. But I had a backup plan: I had fourteen bottles of pills, including three bottles of Tylenol 3s, that I had accumulated. I sat in the driver's seat and started taking the pills, one bottle after another, until there were none left. The next thing I knew, I had blacked out.

When I woke up, I was back at home again in my bed, confused and disappointed. I put the battery back into my phone to call for help, but no sooner had I started dialing than sirens came down my street; the police had arrived. I had driven myself from Cherry Beach to my apartment on Pembroke Street, totally oblivious to the fact that I was driving.

It was midnight when I put the battery back into my phone. As I was leaving my apartment to meet the police at the front door, a neighbour told me that I had smashed my truck into the back fence behind our building. I went out to the police and the last thing I remember was staring up at the six lights inside of the ambulance.

I woke up ten days later in the hospital, again having overdosed on enough drugs that I should have died. The emergency doctor said the Tylenol 3s alone were enough to cause complete liver failure. He suggested it was a miracle that I was alive and that I should start to appreciate life. I ended up at the hospital for the next two weeks on the 17th floor of St. Michael's.

Exposing myself to complete strangers in the hospital meant I had to endure a lot of negative comments and mispronunciation of my name and people using the wrong pronouns. I wish I could have reconnected with my kids earlier, back in July of 2009, when things began to spiral out of control, but alas, that was not my decision to make. It seemed Maria had more control over the children than I could have imagined, and she called the shots from our home in Sutton.

If I think back and remember all the times in the hospital, in support groups, and in church crying uncontrollably, I realize I must have been a sight to see. Here I was, a 6'2 trans woman, usually in a dress, sobbing uncontrollably because of my situation—not something that people expect to see of someone my size. The manic states I had of needing to die, resonated throughout my life as a woman. Creating all these documentaries and interviews, and even this book, is my way of recording for history the change in my life and how getting human rights makes everyone safer in the trans community.

Since 2009, the word 'trans' has gone from being virtually obscure to becoming a household word by 2019. Almost everyone has had to learn and adjust their way of thinking to understand the risks for people in our transgender community.

I believe for the most part people have come a long way to becoming empathetic to our need for acceptance and understanding gender expression and gender identity.

I'm not sure if we would be where we are today if not for the activists lobbying for trans rights throughout the world to promote acceptance. Or, on the other hand, would we have seen the recent backlash of hate by those who insist that gender-variant people are evil? The idea that God hates transgender people is thrust upon us. What I do know is I transitioned throughout the time that the world was getting introduced to transgender people like me. Like a tidal wave hitting society, I rode my surfboard on that wave to the place I am now, safe and sound and living a quasi-normal life in dresses.

A mental health diagnosis can seem scary to others, but what's really scary is living with a mental health diagnosis and taking all the medications that doctors prescribe to try to help alleviate our suffering. They all come with so many side effects. I honestly can't tell you how many different medications they tried on me. Some, in the hospital, were experimental; some, prescribed by various doctors, were detrimental, and some I took really did make a difference. Of all the cocktails of pharmaceuticals that were designed to help me sleep and help me want to live, I'm now down to twelve drugs, and my life is getting easier because my mind is clearer.

The main drug that helped me do better was seeing my children again. It's amazing that Maria had so much control over keeping us isolated from each other for over a decade and no one would stop her. Parental alienation syndrome is genuine and very detrimental to society as a whole, not to mention the family members themselves. The courts need to address this problem before it gets out of control.

Once, while I was an inpatient at CAMH in the fall of 2017, I organized a play party for everyone on the floor, to show the staff that sometimes drugs aren't needed to help us feel better. "Daddy" got the supplies I needed for us to have what looked like a birthday party or slumber party in the common room. We had chips, candy, and juice boxes. Almost everyone on the floor participated and had a great time. The nurses commented that that was the quietest night on the floor that they could remember, with everyone just chilling together, coloring, listening to kids' music, and playing with dolls and Teddy Bears. I've had many occasions where I've witnessed this effect on people. It's nice to see everyone playing along together and forgetting their troubles. I hope you'll try it and see the transformation for yourself.

Despite being at the hospital to receive care, I often went out of my way to make other people's stay much better. I remember once, a young woman came in because she had spent $700 that her grandmother had given her to pay her credit card off on drugs, which made her suicidal. I felt really sad that she would want to end her life over $700, so we slipped out on a day pass to go and pay off her credit card. The next day she was okay to go home again. On other occasions, I would intervene in patients' lives by helping them understand that communication is the best remedy to resolve family issues. I liked spending time with others, talking through problems and looking for simple solutions. I understand that a lot of mental health issues have very complex solutions, but I also understand that there are times when just being a friend to someone in need is enough to give them hope. It is my hope that the doctors, nurses, and patients that I've met through my various hospital stays, will see themselves in these stories that I've described and shared here in this book.

Chapter 22
C-26 Canadian Charter of Rights and Freedoms, June 2017

All the work and suffering that I, and others like me, went through was almost worth it because on June 19, 2017, after years of lobbying and trying to get transgender rights, Prime Minister Justin Trudeau's government added Gender Identity and Gender Expression to the list of protected grounds in the Canadian Charter of Rights and Freedoms.

Bill C-16 sparked a national debate, but actually, it brought federal laws up to date with already-established provincial transgender human rights protections, such as Ontario's Toby's Law.

Bill C-16 has become part of a larger conversation surrounding gender, pronoun use, freedom of speech, and the rights of transgender and gender-diverse Canadians. Unfortunately, there's been a backlash against trans people because those on the extreme right believe that talking about gender expression and the use of puberty blockers is somehow harming young trans people. They couldn't be further from the truth: language and dialogue create clarity for children who may already be confused.

Puberty blockers, or pre-puberty medical intervention, delay the onset of typical puberty changes to the body until after the client is old enough to decide for themselves which gender they will choose to live in. Transitioning is made much simpler when the client does not have to contend with signs of puberty such as breasts, menstruation, facial hair, voice changes, and changes in bone structure, typically identifying a person as male or female.

When politicians decide that teachers need to "out" trans kids to parents who may be transphobic themselves, they're putting those children in danger.

Bill C-16 added the words "gender identity or expression" to three places in Canadian law.

First, it was added to the Canadian Human Rights Act, joining a list of identifiable groups that are protected from discrimination. Characteristics such as age, race, sex, religion, and disability, among others. People in all of these groups are protected and benefit from getting these human rights.

Second, it was added to a section of the Criminal Code that targets hate speech, which is defined as advocating genocide and the public incitement of hatred against identifiable groups, where it joins other identifiable groups. This law may be used against those MPs who are using proposed legislation to bully kids. In the end, this will protect vulnerable minorities who are already struggling with their gender identity.

Third, it is included in a section of the Criminal Code dealing with sentencing for hate crimes. If there's evidence that an offence is motivated by bias, prejudice, or hate, it can be taken into consideration by the courts during sentencing. I may test this by bringing a case over my experiences in the legal system because I should have been protected under Toby's law in Ontario in 2015.

The fact that Bill C-16 enshrines the rights of transgender or gender-diverse Canadians by including them under human rights and hate-crime laws has sparked a huge backlash by politicians and leaders on the far right. Critics have suggested that the law would penalize citizens who do not use specific pronouns when referring to gender-diverse people. However, the Criminal Code says misusing pronouns alone would not constitute a criminal act. Would it cover a situation where an individual repeatedly refuses to use a person's chosen pronoun? It might, but after seeing the lengths that U of T professor Jordan Peterson went to in misgendering students in his classes, for example, it is unlikely that the courts would make a decision even for these extreme cases.

If you're not sure, ask a trans-person how they wish to be addressed. Use 'they' if you don't know which pronoun is preferred. Simply referring to the person by their chosen name is always a respectful approach.

The Canadian Human Rights Act is a federal act — its scope includes the federal government itself and First Nations governments, as well as federally regulated employers, such as banks and telecommunications companies.

Most other situations are covered under the Provincial Charter of Rights Act, stating that when it comes to employment, education, and housing, transgender people have the right to file a human rights complaint if they feel they have been mistreated because of their gender identity or expression.

Although things are going in the right direction, there are provinces that rule that it's a parent's right to decide if their children can present as a different gender from that which was assigned at birth, change their name or pronouns, or seek gender-affirming therapy. Many parents treat their children harshly if they identify as transgender, and allowing schools to give all the power and responsibility to the parents may put transgender students in harm's way. If young people felt that they were safe to discuss their gender identity with their parents, they would do so before they took the issue to school. It's those students who are afraid to tell their parents because of what may happen to them whose gender identity needs to remain a secret in order to keep them safe from harm.

We will continue to work on advocating for the rights of people to self-identify, free from violence and discrimination.

One big thing that has happened since starting the fight for gender rights is that there is more public dialogue, which has led to more people coming out and identifying as transgender. The numbers back in 2007 made it seem like one in 300,000 people was transgender, but now, with the increase in dialogue, one could argue that the numbers are closer to one in 100. Through dialogue, we get language that we can identify with that makes us feel safe being who we are.

When I was a child, I didn't understand who I was because it was never talked about. I heard what people said about 'tomboys' and boys who were 'sissies,' and all the language was hurtful. Now that we have the words, and the understanding, it is less likely that anyone changing their gender identity today will feel the need to harm themselves, be anxious or depressed, or die by suicide. Education on trans identities is saving lives—period.

I hope that the dialogue continues and that eventually, those who are adamantly opposed to protection for transgender people will see that expressing ourselves does not hurt others but makes our lives worth living.

Chapter 23
Chris's Visit, 2019

Without my children in my life, I could not go on living.

No number of pills, no amount of therapy and no amount of assurance could convince me that life without my kids was worth it. So, once again, I found myself in the hospital, this time at St. Joseph's Hospital in Parkdale. While I was there, a doctor had arranged to have my son Christopher come in to visit me. I was having a rough time, and it was the middle of October, so the kids were back at school, and everyone was getting ready for Halloween. I tried doing some crafts in the therapy groups, but they didn't help me feel any better. I spent most of my time crying in my room, rocking my head back and forth in the bed.

On October 17, 2019, just before supper, my nurse came into my room to tell me that my son was there. My heart started racing and she told me to calm down and that he was talking to the doctors and getting informed as to what to expect. She told me that she was instructed to sedate me so I wouldn't be overwhelmed by his visit. I started crying with tears of joy and I just wanted to go out and give him a hug. She told me I would have to wait until he was done with my doctors, which took over an hour.

I walked into the visitors' room and there was Christopher sitting at a table, looking up at me. My eyes filled up with tears, and I started to cry uncontrollably. He stood up and we hugged for what seemed like an eternity. It had now been almost eleven years since I had last seen him. He was a grown man with a full beard and a family. I'm not sure what we talked about; the drugs got the better of me. I do know that he said that we would keep in touch and we would start to visit more often but that we would take baby steps. I agreed with him that that was a good way to do it but I also wanted so badly to go home and meet his wife and kids. I don't remember anything after he had left, I just knew he had left me with a case of honey from his bees that I gave out to the nurses in the nursing station.

Christopher and Isabelle, his wife, had three little girls. Chris told me that one day, his daughter returned from school and told her mother that she had learned that boys and girls can change. Isabelle asked her, "What do you mean?"

She said, "Boys can be girls and girls can be boys."

Isabelle asked her how that made her feel, and she responded with, "Mhhh, it's okay."

At that point, Isabelle and Christopher thought that if this little four-year-old girl could accept transgender people, then maybe they should have a talk with Chris's dad and try to open up the dialogue.

Holding On by a Thread

That little girl saved my life; literally, she saved my life. Since Chris visited, I've had regular phone calls and text messages with them that started off slow in the beginning but gradually became biweekly events. He lived in a small house on a large property in Ottawa and had no room for visitors, but he was open to visiting with me whenever they came down as a family to Toronto. Unfortunately, at this time, Covid-19 came along and the whole country was in lockdown. This went on for over a year, but during that time, he started to talk to his siblings about me, their transgender father. He slowly convinced Robert to make a point of coming down to visit me and get to know me. Robert came down to my apartment on March 21, 2021, for a short visit. Now you need to know that the last time I'd seen Robert had been twelve years earlier, when he was only eleven years old. I stood out front and watched the white pickup truck pull up and a twenty-three-year-old man stepped out with a big grin on his face. He said in a very low baritone voice, "Hi Dad!"

This set me back because the last time I heard his voice it had been the voice of a child, not the deep voice of a grown man. I showed him my apartment and he stayed for a nice visit. Eventually, he said he had to go again but that we would keep in touch, which we did. I now had two of my kids back in my life—one married with three kids and the fourth on the way, and the other single and happy to have me back into his life.

Robert lived in Sutton and shared a house with his brother Peter and Peter's girlfriend, Samantha (Sam). Peter and Robert had bought the house as an investment, but now that Peter and Sam were getting married, Peter bought out Robert, who'd stayed on as a tenant. Robert was saving up his money to buy a house of his own. I would meet Robert one more time when I visited him up near Sutton, but not at his house, and I asked him if the next time we met, I could come to his house and meet Peter and Sam. He said he would check with them and get back to me.

Peter and Sam were willing to meet me, which was amazing news, so by June 6, 2021, I'd reconnected with three of my boys, two of my daughters-in-law, and four of my grandkids. To my surprise, when I was at Peter's house, chatting and having a good time, a car pulled into the driveway, and it turned out to be my daughter Nicole with her two boys, Finley and Elliot. This was to become such an amazing day in my memory. Meeting my two grandsons for the first time and getting to see Nicole after twelve years was a joy, and my heart was overflowing with love.

I started talking to all of them on a regular basis over the phone and visiting once in a while. The boys help me with favors, such as Peter getting stuff from Adrian's house in his pickup truck. And, in the summer of 2022, Robert came down to my friends Davina and Doris's house and built their fireplace for them. Robert is a stonemason and a volunteer firefighter. Peter is a mechanic and a firefighter, and Sam is an elementary school teacher. Such a beautiful family, and slowly, I would see my grandkids on a regular basis, and they would get to know me as Opa.

One time, when I was visiting Nicole at her house, she answered the door and said, "Hi, Dad! Come on in." Then she turned to her husband, Kyle, and said calmly, "My dad is here. Could you make HER a coffee?" What an amazing thing to hear. I was still her dad, but in her mind, she would use female pronouns when introducing me; she saw me as the woman I am and made me feel great.

A year and a half has passed, and Christopher has since moved to a larger house in the Ottawa area, a farm with many extra bedrooms. In October 2022, I had my first weekend at his house with my daughter-in-law and grandkids. I brought my cat along and the kids loved Mykoto and noted that he looked like their cat Paisley. The kids and I did crafts, we played with the animals in the barn, and they regaled me with all their stories and shared gifts with me. Chris and I toured his farm with his girls, and later we would install some windows in his barn. What an amazing family. Chris is still a beekeeper, selling his honey under the label Lullabee Honey, but now he has two pigs, a dog, three cats, and a whole bunch of chickens to go along with the bees.

Christopher and his daughter checking the bees

I can't tell you how great it feels to have four of my kids back in my life with their spouses and their children. I hope and pray that soon, my other three kids will also come around and invite me into their lives. I would love it for us to be a complete family again.

Also, in 2019, I began taking sewing lessons at the Toronto school board's adult learning center in Etobicoke. I joined the sewing class as a beginner and registered under my male name, Paul Wolscht, which would be the name they would find on my school transcripts. On the first day, I went to class wearing a dress and responded to the attendance when they called out my name. No one said anything about how I presented, and everyone was really nice to me. But a few times in the first few lessons, when I made a mistake sewing, I would utter under my breath, "Stefonknee…"

Our teacher, Elsy, asked me who this Stefonknee is? I told her that Stefonknee is the name that I have gone by since my transition in 2009, but my school transcripts were still under Paul. Elsy went to the attendance sheet, crossed out Paul, wrote in my name, and told me that Paul was not in the class anymore. She said Stefonknee was now a student in her class. It felt so good that they accepted me for who I was and respected my name and pronouns that I kept taking the course every spring and fall until Covid-19, at which point the school was closed down.

I learned that Elsy would be opening a studio at her house and accepting students once the lockdown was lifted. A year later, I was going to her house and studio to learn more about sewing and embroidery. Elsy McCormick and I have become really good friends over the years, and I've got to know her husband, Robert, really well, too. She knows that sewing is a coping mechanism for me to keep me from becoming depressed or anxious, not to mention that I love sewing. I'm now the proud owner of a sewing machine, a serger, and a Babylock embroidery machine. I love all the friends that I've made at her studio, and we have a great time every Saturday morning. By the way, they make the best coffee in Toronto.

Unfortunately, on April 9, 2021, five police officers knocked on my door at four a.m. As I opened the door, I was surprised to see police officers with rifles drawn pointed at me. They accuse me of shooting my grandmother. It was terrifying looking down the barrel of five rifles, and it triggered me to want to die. I was mad that they had come in the middle of the night and accused me of killing my grandmother when, in fact, she died in 1975. I told them that my grandmother was dead, but she died when I was twelve. They still insisted on coming in to check and see if there was a crime scene.

Later that morning, some neighbours said that the police had knocked on their doors to see if they had heard any gunshots, and they all told me that they had heard nothing throughout the night. I called my superintendent to ask if he had copies of the video from the surveillance cameras, but unfortunately, he said the cameras weren't working. This incident gave me nightmares for months and might have been one of the contributing factors to my being suicidal again. Unfortunately for me, the police reacted negatively to the rumour that people started about me, that I'd shot my grandmother, rather than looking for evidence. That's part of my complex PTSD: I'm afraid that when I hear sirens, they are coming to get me again and turn me into a criminal.

I'm really grateful for all the good things in my life: my children and grandchildren, my friends, and all those who have helped me through the years. I hope and pray that I will continue to progress and get stronger with each day.

Chapter 24
Covid-19

Chris came to visit me at St. Joe's Hospital on October 17, 2019, and things started looking brighter. We had no idea that in just a few months, the pandemic known as COVID-19 would put everyone in lockdown and paralyze the world. For me, this was devastating. Not only did it isolate me from Christopher and his family, but it also isolated me from Adrian, whose advanced age and health meant that being infected could cost him his life.

During this time, I had a very small bubble that included my friends Melissa Hudson, Laura Bennett, and Paul Urbanas. We did not see a lot of each other, but we did stay in contact. We all needed to clamp down and stay home as much as possible to avoid the pandemic spreading to everyone. The possibility of passing on a life-threatening disease scared me and so I complied with all the government restrictions. If we got together, we would wear a mask and visit outside in the fresh air, usually in my backyard. We would social distance ourselves approximately three meters apart and use disinfectant whenever we touched something.

Melissa, Laura, and I started sewing masks for the "Sewing Army" group that was set up to make cloth masks for frontline workers throughout Canada. It was a nice way to keep busy, and it didn't take very long before people were contacting us directly and we were delivering masks all over Toronto. Shipments went coast to coast from Newfoundland as far as Vancouver. They were desperate times and masks had become hard to find, and doing this sewing work made us feel like we were contributing. We sewed a three-layer mask with some cotton in the center to work as a filter. We knew it was filtering better than the two-layer masks because when you breathed through them, the mask would actually move towards your mouth when you inhaled, which gave us confidence that these masks were actually making a difference. But eventually, the government was able to supply N-90 masks to all the hospitals, so our volunteer business started quieting down.

After a few months, the isolation started affecting my mood and I became depressed again. Not only was I isolated again from my family and friends, but also any progress reconnecting with my children and siblings was now impossible.

I had been treated for kidney stones in September 2019, but by January 2020, I could feel another kidney stone and it affected my ability to walk. Because of Covid-19, I couldn't get the stone treated and I quickly fell deeper into depression, so much so that on September 2, 2020, I attempted to take my life by overdosing on insulin.

I called the crisis line to let them know that I was spiraling downwards, and to let them know that I had a plan to end my life.

Their lines were too busy, and I was told by recording that someone would call me back within the next twenty-four hours, so I decided to take three vials of insulin at once and then I left my apartment and wandered the streets that night. I didn't know it, but while I was walking around in the dark a call had been made to first responders to come and find me. Eventually, an ambulance pulled up behind me on the street not too far away from my home and took me to Toronto Western Hospital.

I don't remember too much about my hospital stay except that they were giving me high doses of sugar to combat the effects of the insulin, and they had formed me so I couldn't leave the hospital. Once the form had expired, I quickly got changed into my own clothes and snuck out of the hospital. I made my way back to my apartment, injected all the rest of my insulin, and again left to find a peaceful place to lie down and die. I had made my way close to a cul-de-sac that was isolated on a one-way street and walked along the fence beside the park to find a quiet place to lie down.

As I was walking, a police officer approached me and asked if I was Stefonknee Wolscht. I said yes, not knowing what he could do to help me. The officer led me back to his cruiser and shortly after that, an ambulance arrived and took me back to the hospital. I don't remember getting to the hospital or what happened inside the hospital. I had blacked out and was dissociating, unable to appreciate what I had done. I was frustrated, in pain, and very depressed.

Months later, on my phone, I found a video of me in the hospital talking about needing to go and feed my dog. I didn't have a dog, and I was saying things on tape that weren't true. I realized, once I saw the video that I was really out of it and had no comprehension of what had happened to me. I know from my hospital records that I saw psychiatrists and I was discharged, but I just don't remember talking to anyone or being there the second time.

I was happy to get a call from St. Mike's Hospital to say that they could fit me in in January 2021, to get the kidney stone taken care of. Once the kidney stone was removed, not only was I able to walk normally again but I could also actually start taking deep breaths without being in pain. That went a long way to keeping me from falling back into depression because I felt healthy and stronger again.

In my journal I have a list of doctors who took care of me, but I don't know who they are. I am forever grateful that they were able to put the wheels in motion to not only protect me from myself but to also get the kidney stone pain taken care of.

Not too long after that, I started visiting with Christopher and his family and meeting up with my other children as the lockdown had ended.

Since that last visit to the hospital for depression in September of 2020, I have never felt depressed again and I've never had to call for help about my anxiety. It feels really good to be stable and happy, not afraid of myself.

I Was Thinking of You

I was thinking of you today, where did it all go wrong?
Could we have avoided this long before it got so messed up?
I'll never understand the reasons for what happened.
I wonder if anyone really understands.

I was thinking of you today, could I have made a difference?
You must have struggled continually with decisions.
You had so little time to think things through.
I didn't have to make those choices, or live with the memories.

I was thinking of you today, and all the things I take for granted.
How much were you expecting to pay?
No one can get back what was lost.
Are we able to convince you that it was worth it?

I was thinking of you today, how are you coping?
Did you know that you would suffer so much?
Can anyone really understand the loss, the pain, and the suffering?
I often say a special prayer for you.

I was thinking of you today, but I don't know you.
I thank you, but is that enough?
You paid for my freedom.
Your courage and sacrifice changed our world.

I was thinking of you today.

Chapter 25
The Year 2023

Since the time of my coming out of the closet, until the start of writing this book, I've missed out on five of my children's weddings, the births of ten of my grandchildren, and the funerals for my father and my sister. Those are things I have to live with, that will never change. Those are memories that don't include me and that aren't there to reflect back on. It's hard to think of all that has been lost, but I try to focus on the future and be thankful for all that I have. I'm grateful for having the opportunity to see things differently and to learn from what I've lived through.

On January 30, 2023, the day before I started writing this book, my sister, Monica McCartney, passed away. When I looked at her obituary, my name was missing. I first got a hint that something was wrong when my cousin Linda sent her condolences to our family on Facebook and mentioned everyone except for me. Needless to say, it feels very bad, and that saddens me a lot. I commented on her post that "Monica was like a sister to me."

1w   Like   Reply   1 ❤️

Linda Saul Shantz
I'm so sorry for this loss for you Shawnalee
Wolscht, for her husband Brad & her children,
for Robert Wolscht, Eric Wolscht, Mike
Wolscht, for all of Monica's nieces and
nephews 💔
Godspeed to her 🙏

1w   Like   Reply   3 ❤️👍

Paul Wolscht
Linda Saul Shantz Sorry for your loss,
she was like a sister to me. May she rest
in peace with Mom and Dad

1w   Like   Reply

I felt that I needed to say something, Linda never responded.

In Memory of

Monica McCartney

1961 - 2023

Obituary of Monica McCartney

Monica peacefully passed away at home surrounded by her family on Monday, January 30, 2023. Monica McCartney (nee Wolscht) of Sandford, Ontario at 61 years of age.

Beloved wife of Brad. Loving mom of Ian (Kerry), Christin, Mathew (Belinda) and Adrian (Samantha). Proud oma of Margo. Dear sister of Michael Wolscht, Eric Wolscht, and Robert (Shawna Lee) Wolscht. Monica will also be fondly remembered by her nieces and nephews.

Obituary excluding Paul Wolscht, sad that some things are still hurtful

This was the catalyst to get me to start writing this book as I don't know how many days I have left, and I wanted to share my experiences in some tangible way. It has been quite the adventure, and quite satisfying, to organize my thoughts and put them down on paper. I'm glad that I was given the opportunity to share this with you, the reader.

Holding On by a Thread

When Christopher came to the hospital and promised to stay in contact, he was true to his word. I have since met his wife, Isabelle, and his kids, Amelia, Felicity, Sophia, Martin, and Edith. It's been an amazing few years, and I love them all for bringing hope back into my life and reconnecting me with my other kids. I've seen them numerous times over the years, and I love going to their farm in the Ottawa area. I love them, and I know they love me and accept me for who I am and with all my baggage.

Since COVID-19 ended, I've been reunited with my son Robert, my daughter Nicole and her husband Kyle, and their two boys Finley and Elliot, as well as my son Peter and his wife Samantha (and recently Elora, their new daughter.) We've reconnected many times, and we're all making new memories as one family.

Through my kids who are in my life, I'm working to try and reconnect with my daughters Chavonne and Amanda, and my son Michael. I hope that it won't be long until we are one family again with everyone loving each other like in the past.

I've also recently been reunited with Adrian and have found that our relationship picked up right where it left off before COVID-19. I visit Peterborough often with my cat, Mykoto, and we find it very relaxing and quiet up there. I really appreciate having a place to escape to when the city gets too noisy and hectic.

Stefonknee Wolscht

On October 1, 2023, I was at a Toronto Blue Jays baseball game when I bumped into my brother Mike, his significant other, Janet, and his other friend Otto. That brief introduction led to me visiting Mike at his house in Zephyr, where I met my other brother, Eric. Eric, Mike, Janet, and I had a wonderful afternoon, and we were able to talk about everything and make plans for the future. Any hard feelings were wiped away, and we agreed to stay connected and create new memories together.

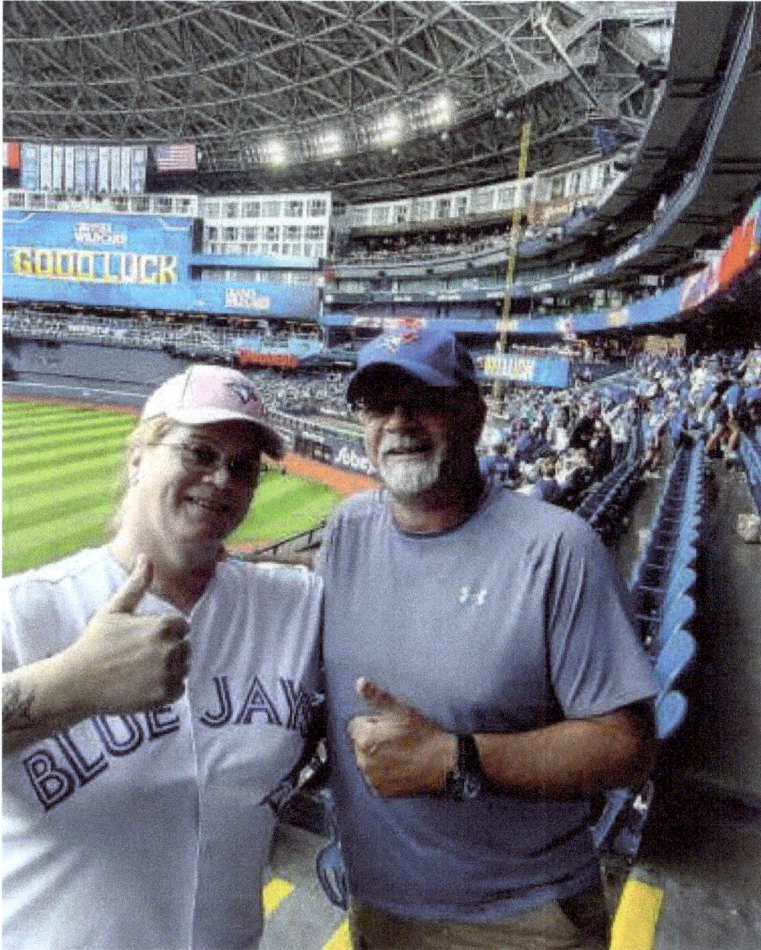

Stefonknee and Mike Wolscht at Blue Jays baseball (October 1, 2023)

On December 9, Mike, Janet, my brother Rob, and his wife, Shawna, came down to Toronto for a Christmas concert (Hark!") at

MCC Toronto, where they met more of my friends. It was a nice reunion, linking all of us to each other.

On January 2, my brother Robert had a cardiac arrest at fifty-two years old and narrowly escaped passing away. All my friends were saddened by the fact that he came so close to dying and prayed for his speedy recovery. I'm glad to announce he's recovered really well. Rob is doing a lot better now and is back at home and I'm able to go and visit with him so that we can celebrate the life we have together.

I've since started being reunited with many of my nieces and my nephews as time allows and I bump into them when I visit my brothers. It's nice to know that the world is becoming more accepting of transgender people, one person at a time.

I cannot express enough how good the love we share for each other feels, and how nice it is to be talking about the future and reminiscing about the past. Slowly, things are getting back to normal and it's almost as if fourteen years of separation never existed. I really love all of my friends and family for sticking by me and accepting me as a trans woman.

It did take a long time to find hope, but in the end, I was successful. I know I went through some rough times—as a lot of people do—and I hope that if you're struggling in darkness, you may find that through reading this book, you can hold on a little longer until you find your hope. Please try not to despair and do look for those rainbows out there when there are rainy days. I really love my life now, and I'm glad that I survived those dark days.

Chris, Finley, Nicole and Stefonknee at MCCT for the first "Non Binary Parent's Day" April 21, 2024

Dash

by Stefonknee Wolscht

Dash, dash, dash, dash is all we know.

Problem with a dash is you can't take it slow.

Take a little dash of this, add a little dash of that,

From a mommy and a daddy and…POOF! That's where you're at.

Let me slow it down, just to bring you up to speed.

A sperm and an egg are really all you need.

The egg sees the sperm, then all you hear is whoa,

Still, one dashes through, there you are, so here we go!

Stefonknee Wolscht

Now you're sitting in your womb, just to multiply and grow,

Mommy tries to puke you out, but her body says no.

So, you wiggle and you squirm, and you kick and you punch,

Cause you're ducking and a' dashing from the crap she ate for lunch.

Pretty soon you gotta dash, dash, dash, now you really gotta try.

Wasn't nine months ago, you were a twinkle in Dad's eye.

So, you pop into the world, get a slap to make ya cry.

Cause they wanna start your dash, though you can't imagine why.

If your poop'n and a' peeing, all you gotta do is cry,

And their running and a' dashing, cause they wanna keep you dry.

They're a' talk'n of your training, as they try to teach you why,

You're a' dashing to be dryer, to the potty with a sigh.

Now they dash you off to school, so you learn to read and write,

Dash you home with books and paper, keeps you up for half the night.

Dash you off to play some hockey, do ballet, and dash you back,

Just to dash you off to school again, with more stuff in your pack.

Now you dash away to college, just to dash away from home,

You say you're dashing off for knowledge, but all you wanna do is roam.

You dash to make more friends, and you dash to get to class,

Not for higher education, but for booze and pot and hash.

After graduation, and the corporate ladder climb,

You dash to get house, spouse, and kids, and not a dime.

Holding On by a Thread

You're dashing and a' dodging as you try to stay afloat,

Cause they got ya where they want ya, dashing round to make you cope.

After forty years of working, dashing back and forth from home,

You get a fancy watch, an RV, and a dashing garden gnome.

You've been dashing all your life, just to settle down for fun,

Now you're a dashing, aging snowbird, dashing south for golf and sun.

Now your body's getting colder as you look on fields of green.

Got a tombstone with your name on it, that's such a peaceful scene.

You're a' floating and a' twirling as your spirit's dashing home,

Between your birthdate and the end…You got a new dash of your own!

Chapter 26

Conclusion

As I've walked the path that is my life, I've learned a lot about human nature and about myself. I've learned that I really did have white male privilege for forty-six years, although admittedly, I didn't learn that until I lost it. Only after losing it did I realize that I did not earn everything I had accomplished in my life; most of it was given to me.

With the help of so many people, we spent the next ten years of my life advocating for human rights and lobbying various levels of government to protect us from discrimination. It was remarkable how quickly we were able to accomplish this.

Unfortunately, since getting trans rights in Canada and drawing awareness to transgender issues throughout the world, there has been a backlash. Conservative governments and right-wing Christian fundamentalists are choosing to attack transgender people, as we seem to be a popular target since drawing attention to ourselves. It's become a way to win votes on the right. I believe that trans people are like the canaries in the coal mines, so to speak, showing that just below the surface, there is a backlash ready to raise its head and crush LGBTQ rights. I think they're coming after trans folk first, and then they will come after everyone else. They have even begun to reverse women's rights in some states of the USA.

"First, they came for the Socialists, and I did not speak out— Because I was not a Socialist. Then they came for the Trade Unionists, and I did not speak out— Because I was not a Trade Unionist. Then they came for the Jews, and I did not speak out— Because I was not a Jew. Then they came for me—and there was no one left to speak for me." Martin Niemöller

These words, written soon after the Holocaust, spoke up against apathy—and for the moral connectedness of all people.

I've learned that love is a fragile thing that can be so hard to find and yet lost so easily, and once it's lost, things can feel hopeless but don't despair because it can come back.

I've also learned that when the chips are down and you have nothing to give back, you'll find out who your true friends are. They are the ones who stick by you despite the fact that you have nothing of value to give them, and they don't care what strangers say about who you are.

I think that I've made huge mistakes in my life, but some of the things that I regret have nothing to do with the choices I made; they were more of a problem with my boundaries. In life, we have to play the cards we're given, and despite being given some really crappy cards at times, there was always something to learn.

I guess something else that I've learned is that despite things feeling extremely hopeless, if you hold on, reach out for help, and give it enough time, then things will turn around. I had given up on finding something to hope for with regard to my isolation from my family and friends. One small step from Christopher, coming back into my life, opened up the door to more people reuniting with me and giving me something to hope for. I pray that anyone experiencing hopelessness and depression can find comfort in the fact that it took eleven years, but my life did turn around and finally got better. I pray that you are cared for when you're not strong enough to take care of yourself.

Life is fleeting. It seems like only yesterday that I was that little boy in grade one looking at the girls on picture day and envying their pretty dresses. I'm now sixty and in the twilight years of my life. Now, making good decisions, lasting impressions, and happy memories is more important than ever. Hopefully to leave the world a bit better than I found it.

I hope you enjoyed spending a little time here with me and will take a moment to reach out to those you love and let them know that you love them. I think it isn't said enough.

This has been quite the ride over the past fifteen years, and I think it's time for me to write my book... (((((((Hugs))))))) Love, Stefonknee

About the Author

Stefonknee Wolscht is a Catholic, transgender woman and advocate known for her inspiring journey in embracing her true identity. She has gained recognition for her story, which highlights the challenges and triumphs faced by transgender individuals.

Stefonknee was born Paul Andrew Wolscht on June 24, 1963, in Scarborough, Ontario, Canada. She grew up in Mount Albert, Ontario and experienced a profound sense of gender dysphoria from a young age. When her wife of twenty-three years asked her to either stop being transgender or leave their family home, Stefonknee moved to Toronto, and despite the challenges she faced, she transitioned in January 2010. Her transition journey included hormone therapy and gender-affirming surgeries. Stefonknee's journey is a source of inspiration for many transgender individuals who may be facing similar struggles.

Stefonknee has become a vocal advocate for transgender rights and awareness. She has participated in numerous speaking engagements and events to share her experiences and raise awareness about the challenges that transgender people often encounter. Her advocacy work has made a positive impact on the LGBTQ+ community, her story has garnered attention from various media outlets, and she continues to be an inspiration to those seeking to live authentically. Her documentary Living 2 Lives, Dying 1000 Deaths (2010), chronicles her early transition from married father of seven to homeless trans woman on her YouTube channel.

Her documentary, Paul Wears Dresses (2014), follows Stefonknee as she is trying to rebuild her life. After losing her home and her family, Stefonknee gives a firsthand account of the many challenges trans people face. In her hometown of Mount Albert, Stefonknee was known as a loving husband and father, a really good mechanic, and a staunch Catholic, but only she knew the truth; at birth, she had been assigned to the wrong gender.

While Stefonknee was struggling with depression and anxiety, she found that play therapy worked wonders to keep her safe when she was suicidal. Unfortunately, the backlash from the community towards her for taking on the persona of a six-year-old girl to escape the harsh realities of her life, was relentless and overwhelming. In December 2014, Stefonknee went into hiding after receiving hundreds of death threats.

She is now reunited with her siblings and most of her children and is able to create new memories for her family and friends as a woman she was always meant to be.

Stefonknee's YouTube Channel

https://youtube.com/@StefonkneeWolscht

Toronto City News

https://toronto.citynews.ca/2016/01/11/transgender-toronto-woman-says-death-threats-forced-her-into-hiding/

www.ingramcontent.com/pod-product-compliance
Lightning Source LLC
Chambersburg PA
CBHW062116020426
42335CB00013B/980